THIS BOOK IS RESPECTIVELY DEDICATED TO THE SAXON OFFICE (HELLO DAVE, RON & HEIDI), GIOVANNI DADOMO, CHRIS COLLING- WOOD, MIKE DEMPSEY AND OUR FAMILIES & FRIENDS.

Printed and bound in Great Britain at The Camelot Press Ltd, Southampton

Cover illustration, layout and design by Rocky Brann, photoset by Nik Lumsden.

ENCYCLOPEDIA METALLICA

BRIAN HARRIGAN AND MALCOLM DOME

Exclusive distributors
Book Sales Limited, 78 Newman Street, London
London W1P 3LA.
Quick Fox, 33 West 60th Street, New York,
N.Y.10023, USA.
Book Sales Pty. Limited, 27 Clarendon Street,
Artarmon, 2064, Australia.

**BOBCAT
BOOKS**

London/New York/Sydney/Tokyo/Cologne

If you're wondering why I, and not some great literary person has been asked to write the forward of this book, it's because myself, and my colleagues in Saxon, we're part of the musical phenomenon that blasted out of this country two years ago — Heavy Metal, Heavy Rock, Hard Rock or just simply Rock. It's obvious to most people that it actually started more than two years ago, but for the sake of details, this was when it first hit the headlines. It's been called many things, some of which were 'Revival' and 'New Wave Of British Heavy Metal'. Quite a few people have tried to pin down and analyse it and have come up with theories as to why it has become so popular again. Even so, bands like Led Zeppelin, Black Sabbath, Deep Purple etc., have always been popular, and it's bands like ourselves — SAXON, and many others (to whom I apologise for not being able to list here) whom the media call the new bands which have come through. In my opinion this happened because people were sick to death of punk, mod and reggae, — of being told what to like, and the press and radio dominating the country with this type of music. Really, it was YOU who were the phenomenon — the Rock Fan. YOU bought the albums, YOU bought the tickets and YOU demanded the music be played. We were all there ready and just waiting for YOU.

P.S. Keep the faith.

BIFF !?

BORN TO BE WILD. UK SCENE '66.'75

Heavy metal was born in 1966. Two remarkable bands were formed that year who were to exert an enormous influence on rock music, an influence which is still felt today.

The bands were Cream and the Jimi Hendrix Experience. While this chapter is devoted to the development of British heavy metal Jimi Hendrix — at least in his early stages — has to be included for four reasons.

His talents were first recognised by an Englishman, former Animals bass guitarist Chas Chandler. He first came to prominence in England. Indeed, while he was busily achieving superstar status in this country most of his native America was unaware even of his existence, let alone his abilities.

Finally Hendrix was, for his first two albums anyway, an integral part of the British scene. He was regarded as a member of the essentially British clique of supreme rock guitarists — Clapton, Beck and Townshend.

Cream were classic British musicians. They were products of the British R&B boom which flowered from the beginning of the Sixties right through to 1968 (transmuted for the latter three years into the Blues Boom).

Thus they are essential in explaining just how it was that heavy metal evolved.

No style of popular music miraculously appears from nowhere. They are all products of what has gone before.

And that, of course, is as true of heavy metal as of anything else. For it to evolve it needed the blues and R&B booms. Those particular movements emphasised technical virtuosity and were perfect environments for extended solos — two facets which were the cornerstones of the first phase of British heavy metal which, for the purposes of this book, has been dated from 1968 to 1975.

So why talk about Cream and the Jimi Hendrix Experience which, after all, were formed in 1966 and folded in 1968 and 1969 respectively?

They were, quite simply, pioneers of heavy metal and pointed the way for the others to follow.

Interestingly, the real flowering of British heavy metal took place in 1968.

In that year the Yardbirds split up and guitarist Jimmy Page found himself possessor of the band's name, as well as live dates already booked and a recording contract. He decided to form the new Yardbirds and hauled in John Paul Jones — whom he knew through session work — and Robert Plant and John Bonham from the Band Of Joy. Who drummer Keith Moon suggested they name themselves Led Zeppelin.

The same year Jon Lord and Ritchie Blackmore had been planning to join a band formed by ex-Searchers drummer Chris Curtis. The scheme fell through and, through the relationship between two businessmen — John Coletta and Tony Edwards — found themselves teamed up with Ian Paice, Nick Simper and Rod Evans.

They moved into a Hertfordshire farmhouse on March 1, rehearsed solidly for two months and emerged as Deep Purple.

Up in Birmingham Ozzy Osbourne, Geezer Butler, Bill Ward and Tony Iommi formed a band called Earth that year. Originally a blues band they

CREAM

changed their name when they found they were being confused by agents with a pop/cabaret group also called Earth. They called themselves Black Sabbath.

Those three bands dominated the first phase of British heavy metal.

But back to 1966 and before. In the R&B, blues and pop bands in Britain during the early and middle Sixties there had been discernible traces of the forthcoming explosion in heavy metal.

The riff-orientated rock songs were one element of the mixture that was to make up the first recognisable heavy metal. The Kinks in their early period, for example, could now be regarded as having dabbled in HM. Their first two hit singles "You Really Got Me" and "All Day And All Of The Night" were dominated by crashing guitar riffs backed up by bass guitar played in unison and powerhouse drumming.

The rhythmic feel of the Spencer Davis Group's "Gimme Some Loving" and "I'm A Man" was another hint of heavy metal to come.

And so on, the list is extensive. Suffice it to say all the elements of HM were there in one form or another. It was left to the Jimi Hendrix Experience and Cream to tie them all together in one strong and distinguishable form.

Ginger Baker had the longest professional career of the three members of Cream. A drummer in a variety of trad jazz bands in the late Fifties he joined Alexis Korner's Blues Incorporated in 1962. The previous drummer, Charlie Watts, had left to join the Rolling Stones.

The bass player in Blues Incorporated was Jack Bruce. A Glaswegian, he too had had a jazz background playing in the Scotsville Jazzband before coming to London to join Korner's band in the same year as Ginger Baker.

The two split, with fellow member Graham Bond to form the Graham Bond Organisation in February, 1963. Bruce left to join John Mayall's Bluesbreakers in 1965 — and that's where Clapton comes into the picture.

Clapton's initial professional career is one riddled with restlessness and dissatisfaction. The first band he was in — the Roosters — split in August 1963. He spent two months in a band called the Engineers and was then invited to join the Yardbirds as lead guitarist. That lasted until March, 1965.

He joined the Bluesbreakers for a short time immediately after but then decided he'd like to go on a world tour with another band, the Glands. He made it as far as Greece and then returned to Britain and the Bluesbreakers — a stay which lasted from the end of 1965 to June 1966.

Jack Bruce had stayed with the Bluesbreakers for only a short time, leaving for a six months stint with Manfred Mann, an R&B-orientated pop band.

Dissatisfaction with the bands they were in, added to a high regard for each other's musicianship, led to Clapton, Baker and Bruce joining together as Cream.

With musical backgrounds such as theirs it would have been unlikely for Cream to have become anything but a blues band. But it was the type of blues they played which was distinctive. It was hard and heavy, leavened with a supreme confidence in themselves and each other which allowed them to improvise extensively — a highly distinctive ability at the time.

While they were loud and muscular on stage at the time their first recorded work — a single "Wrapping Paper" — was remarkably out of character. A soft, quirky and gentle little tune it made no impression on the charts whatsoever.

But then in December 1966 they released "I Feel Free", a powerhouse of a single which set the pattern for their subsequent output. In the same month their first album, *Fresh Cream* was also released. Both records made the charts in January 1967.

Throughout the band's career Cream's music was dominated by the riff, both in life and studio work. Bruce and his co-writer, jazz musician and poet Pete Brown, had an uncanny knack of creating the most memorable riffs topped with almost magical melody lines and lyrics.

However, whether they were reworking standard blues material — Robert Johnson's "Crossroads", Skip James' "I'm So Glad" — or presenting their own songs — "Strange Brew", "Badge", "Sunshine Of Your Love" — Cream were always dripping with power, energy and expertise.

Well — almost always. Occasionally they went on just too damn long, most notably in Ginger Baker's drum solo in "Toad" or, indeed, the general over-extension of "Spoonful".

Generally, though, they were on top form and

the public on both sides of the Atlantic appreciated it. They enjoyed Top Twenty singles in Britain with "I Feel Free", "Strange Brew" and "Badge". They did the same in the States with "Sunshine Of Your Love" and "White Room".

On the album front they were even more successful earning chart placings in Britain and the States with *Fresh Cream* , *Disraeli Gears* , *Wheels Of Fire* — both the studio album and the double studio/live set — and *Goodbye* .

The band split in 1968 due to disagreements and dissatisfaction. Baker and Clapton went on to join Blind Faith while Bruce went solo — eventually joining the disappointing and inferior West, Bruce and Laing with ex-Mountain men Leslie West and Corky Laing, in 1972.

Aside from the latter's year long outing with West and Laing none of Cream really indulged in heavy metal after that, although some might consider the Baker-Gurvitz Army as a type of HM band. Suffice it to say that was another disappointing band.

However, Cream exerted an enormous influence while they lasted.

No-one has had as much influence on heavy metal, however, as Jimi Hendrix. In the wider context of rock he stands alongside the Beatles and Dylan as one of the few true men of genius that the field has produced.

James Marshall Hendrix was born on November 27, 1942, in Seattle, Washington State. He was black, part Mexican and part Cherokee. He taught himself to play guitar at school, influenced strongly

by the blues, and at the age of 19 he enlisted in the American army as a paratrooper. While he was serving he formed a friendship with fellow paratrooper and bass guitarist Billy Cox — with whom he was later to form the Band Of Gypsies.

Hendrix was invalided out of the army after injuring himself in a parachute drop and, on returning to civilian life, took up a career as a professional musician.

He got his grounding as a guitarist with a vast variety of blues, soul and rock and roll bands, backing up artists like Little Richard, B.B. King, Ike and Tina Turner, Sam Cooke and King Curtis.

Hendrix renamed himself Jimmy James and formed a band called the Blue Flames which fixed up a residency at a New York Club called the Café Wha.

Meantime British R&B band the Animals were playing their last American tour. Bass player Chas Chandler had already made the decision to move out of playing and into management and production. It was Chandler who saw Hendrix playing at the Café Wha in the autumn of 1966.

Chandler was not slow to recognise Hendrix's ability as a guitarist. Allied to that, however, Chandler also saw that in his appearance and his actions Hendrix had immense potential as a charismatic character as well.

The ex-Animal has been quoted as saying that Hendrix was wild enough to upset more people than Mick Jagger.

Chandler brought Hendrix to England and teamed him up with bass-player Noel Redding and

drummer Mitch Mitchell, who had previously been with Georgie Fame and the Blue Flames.

The Jimi Hendrix Experience played a series of club gigs in London which caused an immediate sensation. Guitar heroes like Jeff Beck, Eric Clapton and Pete Townshend flocked to see Hendrix in action.

Hendrix's major breakthrough, however, came with his appearance on the television programme Ready, Steady, Go. That was in December, 1966 just before the end of the three year existence of what was probably the best TV rock programme ever. It was required viewing for anyone interested in music and anyone who made an impact on Ready, Steady, Go was assured of national attention. Hendrix was like a bombshell.

Initially it was his appearance that grabbed attention — he was black, wore exotic clothes and had frizzed out hair which looked as though his scalp had just exploded. Then the guitar work got to you. Hendrix drew sounds out of the guitar which no-one had ever imagined existed.

His first single, ''Hey Joe'', made the charts in January 1967 and eventually rose to number six. His first album, ''Are You Experienced'' charted in Britain five months later.

Before that album had been released the Jimi Hendrix Experience had enjoyed two more hit singles — ''Purple Haze'' and ''The Wind Cries Mary''.

In June 1967 Hendrix and his band appeared at the first ever rock festival, held in Monterey, California. On the bill as well were the Who, Eric

11

Burdon, the Byrds, Janis Joplin, Jefferson Airplane, Otis Redding and dozens of others. Hendrix's performance at that event established him in the States where, previously, his status had been minimal compared with that in Britain.

Subsequently he and his band were booked for a tour of the States with the Monkees. Hendrix was apparently thrown off the tour which, far from hurting his reputation, enhanced his status as something of an anti-hero.

At the end of 1967 the Experience had their second album released — *Axis: Bold As Love* It was a superb set and an excellent follow-up to *Are You Experienced?* . Where the first had shown Hendrix and his band as a mighty engine of power and imminent destruction "Axis" rounded out their image — it showed Hendrix as a subtle and brilliant composer and guitarist, capable of reflecting gentleness as well as frenzy.

On stage, of course, Hendrix was something of a maniac. He smashed his guitar, set fire to it, played it behind his back, made love to it, played it with his teeth — and, at the same time, coaxed out of it the heaviest music ever heard at that time.

With the benefit of 20/20 hindsight it's possible to see the beginning of Hendrix's end at the start of 1968. There were arguments within the band, notably between Hendrix and Redding. This wasn't helped by a gruelling tour schedule which the band was committed to.

But Hendrix was making money, and good music too. The band's third album *Electric Lady-land* , which also featured a host of guest artists like Stevie Winwood, Al Kooper and Buddy Miles, was a powerful double set. In addition Hendrix achieved his first Top Twenty hit in the States with his version of Dylan's "All Along The Watchtower", which also charted in the UK.

If 1968 was a mixed year the following one was confused and frustrating. The man who had discovered Hendrix, Chas Chandler, was squeezed out and the Jimi Hendrix Experience was broken up — the quarrels between Hendrix and Redding having come to a head. Hendrix had set up his own recording studio, Electric Ladyland, and was spending an immense amount of money on getting into viable operation. In addition Hendrix had attracted an enormous retinue of hangers-on who got in the way of his work and helped him to spend his money.

But there were good moments too. He played the Newport Festival with Mitch Mitchell and Billy Cox and a month later in August he reached what some would rate the pinnacle of his live career — his performance at Woodstock Festival.

If Monterey had made Hendrix a star Woodstock made him a superstar. The high point of a cataclysmically powerful set was Hendrix's performance on "The Star Spangled Banner". The whole event is immortalised on film and even now the Hendrix show stands supreme.

The end of 1969 saw Hendrix dropping Mitch Mitchell and forming the Band of Gypsies with Billy Cox and Buddy Miles. They recorded one live album — titled *Band of Gypsies* — but their career was spectacularly short. On only their second gig, in New York's Madison Square Garden, Hendrix left the stage within minutes of the show starting. The band was finished.

In 1970 Hendrix recorded his last album, played his last festival and performed on his last tour. The album was *Cry Of Love* the festival was the Isle Of Wight — with Billy Cox and Mitch Mitchell back in the fold.

On September 18 of that year Hendrix died in London. He choked to death on his own vomit.

Both Cream and Hendrix were short lived in their own ways — Cream professionally and Hendrix literally. Their recorded output was not particularly large but their effect on other musicians and future rock artists was disproportionately large.

Hendrix first and foremost took guitar playing and stage outrage to new and unsuspected heights — he was pyrotechnic in both areas.

Cream demonstrated immense ability individually as guitarist, bass guitarist and drummer and showed, furthermore, that a band as a whole could be greater than its parts.

However, while Hendrix and Cream were foremost among the pioneer heavy metal artists they were by no means operating in isolation in Britain.

The Yardbirds are worth a mention if only for the three major guitarists the band boasted during its five years — Eric Clapton, Jeff Beck and Jimmy Page. They were essentially an R&B band although during the last half of 1966 there must have been strong traces of HM about them with Page and Beck swopping guitar solos every night on stage.

Aside from the personnel of the band the Yardbirds also had another role to play in the heavy metal saga. Their influence on American musicians, alongside that of the Who and Kinks, gave that country's budding HM scene a flying start.

Jeff Beck himself had an enormous reputation in the States gained first with the Yardbirds and then with his own Jeff Beck Group which featured Rod Stewart on vocals, Ron Wood on bass, Mick Waller on drums and Nicky Hopkins on piano. The Beck Group lasted from 1967 to 1969 at which point Beck decided to form a band with American heavy metallists Tim Bogert and Carmine Appice who had previously been in Vanilla Fudge — responsible for one of the great thrashing singles of all time with "You Keep Me Hanging On".

Unfortunately that scheme was dropped when Beck had a car crash and put himself out of action for 18 months. Bogert and Appice had formed Cactus by this time so Beck collected a second Jeff Beck Group which featured, notably, Cozy Powell on drums. They made two albums before Beck disbanded the outfit. Cactus had also folded and so Beck, Bogert & Appice was formed in 1972 with their first album being released the following year.

It was a disappointing band and never made much impression on Britain although they garnered something of a reputation in the States. Beck did little worthy of attention after BB&A folded.

On the more manic fringe 1967 saw the emergence of the inimitable Arthur Brown — or, to give his band its full title, The Crazy World Of Arthur Brown. The band initially consisted of Vincent Crane on keyboards and Crachen Theaker on drums. Later Theaker was replaced by Carl Palmer

The band's music was pure mayhem, insane thrashing which almost inevitably on every song ended up on a crashing climax of noise and destruction. Brown reached his zenith with "Fire", written by himself and Crane. On stage Arthur wore bizarre headgear which he would set on fire. The opening, stentorian line of the song, which was a hit in Britain and the States, boasts one of the daftest and most memorable lyrics in rock: "A AM THE GOD OF HELL FIRE . . . AND I BRING YOU . . . FIRE!!!"

The pomp rock side of heavy metal was taking its first faltering steps in the shape of the Nice in 1967. The band consisted of Keith Emerson (organ), Blinky Davison (drums), Lee Jackson (bass) and Davis O'List (guitar and vocals).

They were formed as a backing band for one hit wonder girl singer P.P. Arnold in 1967 but it took them little time to make an impression in their own right with their classically orientated, keyboard dominated works like Dylan's "She Belongs To Me" and Dave Brubeck's "Rondo".

O'List left after the first album, *Thoughts Of Emerlist Davjack*, and on the following album, *Ars Longa, Vita Brevis* Emerson showed his complete mastery of keyboards establishing himself as the focal point of the band.

Their third album was their most ambitious — the *Five Bridges Suite*. After the release of that the band folded and Emerson went on to form a band with Carl Palmer and Greg Lake, but more of them later.

The Nice played a major part in the development of the pomp-rock school of heavy metal and certainly Emerson's influence was enormous.

However, it might be argued that it was also a bad influence since it pointed the way for so many keyboard players and bands to dabble in the sterile area of marrying rock with classical music, a field in which few experiments have succeeded.

Nevertheless, in their time the Nice came up with some exciting music and Emerson must be regarded as one of the very best keyboard technicians. He also demonstrated that keyboardists didn't have to sit down in a docile fashion behind their instrument while the guitarists had all the fun breaking things up. He stabbed his Hammond, kicked it, rocked it about and (rather bravely, I always thought) buggered about with its electrics to produce the most extra-ordinary sounds.

Let's move to 1968 now and concentrate on the three most important bands in the history of British heavy metal: Black Sabbath, Led Zeppelin and Deep Purple.

Sabbath in the beginning consisted of Tony Iommi, Bill Ward, Geezer Butler and Ozzy Osbourne. They were originally called Earth and played blues and jazz numbers around their home town of Birmingham. The four members had known each other at school and to them it seemed that forming a band was a natural course. Certainly there was little else for them to do in the depressed inner-city slum of Aston.

They were managed by Birmingham record company owner and entrepreneur Jim Simpson and it was through him that they embarked on a series of regular and frequent tours around the German night-club circuit. It was the same round of gigs that the Beatles had done at the beginning of the Sixties and, like the Beatles, Sabbath learnt their

DEEP PURPLE

craft there.

It was probably there and in similar places in Britain — like Birmingham's Henry's Blueshouse that Sabbath developed their penchant for playing loud music. With an audience seemingly intent on ignoring the band there would have been no simpler course than to turn up the volume and make them pay attention.

Sabbath, or Earth as they were, did well enough on those Hamburg club dates. In 1969 they broke the house record at the notorious Star Club and were re-booked five times that same year. Tony Iommi told me some years ago: "We had to do so many sets every night we started devoting one whole set to a drum solo by Bill and maybe another to a guitar solo by me. We even got Geezer to do a bass solo one night."

That year Iommi was offered a gig in the embryonic Jethro Tull and he accepted. It would have been a killing blow to the band — but Iommi was back within two weeks where he felt more at home musically and socially.

Earth changed their name to Black Sabbath in 1969. Agents had been mistaking them for a cabaret band for some time but the last straw came when the Sabbath/Earth found themselves playing to a company's annual dinner where the guests expected to be entertained to waltzes and jive. The name change came from a song recently written by the band which, as Ozzy recalls, was penned as an antidote to the peace and love idea which was still floating around them. In characteristic style Osbourne said the band were sick of that notion and decided to write about the world as they, the band, thought it was.

In February 1970 the album *Black Sabbath* was released.

The album, which took two days and cost £600 to record, was unveiled on Friday the 13th, amid a whole load of hype and propaganda hinting at Sabbath's supposed affection for the occult and black magic.

The mixture of this stance and the unrelenting power of the music itself proved irresistible to a large sector of the public. Despite being ignored by the press and the radio *Black Sabbath* smashed into the British charts and stayed there for three months.

Sabbath were eventually hailed as the last of the underground bands, having succeeded on the strength of word of mouth alone, and were also noted as the last of the bands to make it via the German night-club circuit.

They were still working in that field when their album was going up the charts. Geezer Butler remembers looking at the charts in the music papers from Britain and thinking how well the band were playing, the same ones that they'd been doing the year before. He found it hard, he once said, to believe that the Black Sabbath in the charts and the Black Sabbath he was in were one and the same band.

However, in September 1970 the band released a single and an album, both "Paranoid" which irrevocably established them in Britain. Both were a reaffirmation of their musical stance and received an overwhelming public response.

At that same time Sabbath embarked on their first tour of the United States. It was a series of campus dates and it came as a surprise to the band that they were received as well, if not better, by American audiences compared with their British counterparts. From then until 1975 Sabbath continued on a simple and straightforward, if gruelling, career.

In 1971 they brought out *Masters of Reality* the following year it was *Black Sabbath Vol 4* and all the time they were touring constantly all over the world.

Then along came 1973 and the release of what is the best album that Black Sabbath have ever made and, in many minds, the definitive heavy metal collection — "Sabbath, Bloody Sabbath".

This finally marked their inexorable progress to the front ranks of the really big bands. It was also the inevitable blockbuster result of the music they had been making up to that point. It consisted of thunderous sounds, occult concepts, well-written and direct songs and excellent production. Sabbath had reached their peak.

July, 1975, saw the release of *Sabotage* and the band's first appearance at New York's massive and prestigious Madison Square Garden. It was a sell-out within a few days.

Sadly the problems started drawing in around the end of 1975 and the beginning of 1976. The band, now managed by Patrick Meehan, were sued by their original manager, Jim Simpson for breaking their contract. They finally settled their differences. Sabbath decided to look after their own affairs.

The management side, allied to their insistence on maintaining a heavy work schedule, writing their own songs, doing their own production, placed enormous strains on the band.

The inevitable happened in 1977 when Ozzy Osbourne quit Black Sabbath. For many this seemed the point when Sabbath were on the way out. Osbourne was considered — rightly or wrongly — the very image of Sabbath. He had built up a unique rapport with audiences throughout the world and this complete identification between Osbourne and the fans was reckoned to be one of the major factors in Sabbath's success.

However Butler, Iommi and Ward decided to continue as Black Sabbath and brought in former Savoy Brown member Dave Walker — also from Birmingham — as a replacement singer. It didn't work out, however, and when Osbourne indicated his desire, some months later, to rejoin the band Walker was sent on his way with the rock and roll equivalent of a golden handshake.

However, something had changed in the band's internal relationship with the departure of Osbourne and his return to the fold lasted just six months. He was out again and announcing that he was to pursue a solo career.

This time the remaining members of Sabbath decided to find an established front man for their band and came up with Ronnie James Dio, formerly lead singer with Ritchie Blackmore's Rainbow and the possessor of a strong stage persona and an astonishingly powerful voice. That's how it remains today.

RITCHIE BLACKMORE

Ozzy meantime has formed Ozzy Osbourne's Blizzard Of Oz with former Uriah Heep drummer Lee Kerslake, ex-Rainbow bass guitarist Bob Daisley and guitarist Randy Rhodes. There was some public acrimony exchanged between Ozzy and the rest of Black Sabbath but remarkably little compared with other bust-ups, in other bands.

Sabbath went on to produce an album with Dio called *Heaven And Hell* while Ozzy came up with one titled *Blizzard Of Oz*

By all acounts Sabbath have retained both their musical identity and their following and Osbourne appears to be doing just as well with his new outfit.

While Sabbath had something of a hard time throughout their career Deep Purple, in comparison, endured some cataclysmic moments. However, in a period of seven years they made some spectacularly good music and, since their demise in 1976, have given rise to a trio of fine contemporary bands — Whitesnake, Rainbow and Gillan.

But first, the early days. Most seasoned of the original members was keyboard player Jon Lord. He'd been at drama college in London but on leaving in 1961 failed to get any work for two years. He joined a band featuring Art Wood — brother of Ronnie Wood — which lasted for eight singles, one album and four years. The first members of the Artwoods to leave was drummer Keef Hartley. Lord followed suit in 1967 and did session work for eight or nine months.

He joined the Flowerpot Men's backing band where he met the original Purple bass player, Nick Simper. Lord and Simper also met guitarist Ritchie Blackmore at this stage.

Blackmore probably equalled Lord in experience having been a session guitarist since his middle teens. He'd also played in a variety of small-time bands as well as backing Heinz and Screaming Lord Sutch.

He was playing in Hamburg with Sutch when he was invited to join Purple. That invitation came as a result of having met Lord and drummer Ian Paice. Paice had been playing since the early Sixties in this country and in Europe. Paice met Blackmore on a boat going to Italy in 1967 and again at the Star Club, Hamburg later that year. Blackmore had wanted Paice to join him in a band but the drummer refused figuring he was earning good money and didn't want to go into a risky venture.

However, in 1968 Paice answered an advertisement in the music press and found himself auditioning for Deep Purple. It had been Blackmore's idea to get Paice into the band but he had lost touch with him — the advert was a final attempt to find him. The ad also attracted singer Rod Evans.

Purple took off instantly in the States. Their first album, *Shades Of Deep Purple*, was released in September 1968. It included the single "Hush", a heavy version of the Bobby Goldsboro composition, which made the top five in America.

June, 1969 saw the release of the second album, *Blood Of Taliesyn*, which like its predecessor was a hit in America. So were two tracks from the album released as singles — Neil Diamond's "Kentucky Woman" and the Ike and Tina Turner classic "River Deep, Mountain High".

As might be gathered Deep Purple were by no means the band then that they have since come to be recognised. They were essentially a pop band, happily adopting any musical identity and adapting any song that might be a commercial success.

This began to change, though, in September with the release of their third album *Deep Purple* Most of the songs were highly riff-orientated with the notable exception of "April" which boasted Jon Lord's string and woodwind arrangements. These two aspects, the classical and the metallic, were to be cornerstones of the band's work in the future.

The third was the last album to feature Rod Evans and Nick Simper. They were jettisoned in favour of two members of Episode Six, Roger Glover and Ian Gillan who were thought to be better suited for Purple's attempt to become a consistently heavier band.

Evans went off to the States to try and form a band with a couple of former members of Cactus while Semper formed an outfit called Warhorse.

Gillan had been introduced to Blackmore by a mutual friend, Mick Underwood who was drummer in Episode 6. When Gillan went along to the Purple audition Glover went too.

One of their first live recordings was a concert with the Royal Philharmonic Orchestra at the Royal Albert Hall in London. This occasion was the premiere of Jon Lord's *Concerto For Group And Orchestra*. It was recorded live and released four months later to an extremely mixed response. Some critics rated it as a step forward in the natural evolution of "progressive" rock. Most others thought it was ill-advised. It certainly didn't do particularly well commercially and now, ten years later, it doesn't stand up too strongly. Nonetheless the band considered it a valid experiment.

It was over-shadowed by the band's subsequent album, the first rock outing with Glover and Gillan. *Deep Purple In Rock* was released in June, 1970 and was a monster smash all over the world. It established Deep Purple in Britain as a major attraction and stayed in the charts in that country for over a year. The album featured, among others, "Speed King" and "Child In Time". A track recorded at the same time — "Black Night" — but left off the album was released as a single and became the band's biggest single success in Britain.

By the end of 1972 Deep Purple had released three more albums — *Fireball*, and *Made In Japan*. They had also followed the classic route of gigging constantly all over the world. In November of that year Jon Lord reckoned the band had done 100 plus concerts in 12 months. In classic fashion that schedule had placed tremendous pressures on the band. Their contract with EMI stipulated two albums a year which proved to be one hell of a struggle for the band to fulfil.

It was no surprise when Gillan and Glover left at the beginning of 1973. Gillan had business interests to look after while Glover complained of ill-health plus a desire to get into production.

Glen Hughes of Trapeze was brought in on bass. Purple had seen the band playing at the Whiskey A Go Go in Los Angeles in 1972 and had rated him then. His induction was no problem.

But getting a new singer was more difficult.

One of the favoured names was Paul Rodgers but contractual problems and an unwillingness on Rodgers' part "not to let people down" aborted that move.

Purple went on the audition trail. David Coverdale who was working in a clothes shop in Redcar by day and playing in a band called the Fabulosa Brothers at night sent a three year old demo tape to Purple HQ in London. He received a call inviting him down. He joined the band at the end of 1973. Glover and Gillan had gone out on a rough album, titled *Who Do We Think We are*, which Jon Lord was later to describe as a "bullshit album".

However the next albums were considerably stronger and showed that Hughes and Coverdale had a revitalising and novel effect on Purple. *Burn* had a degree of funk about it which was extended by *Stormbringer*. That year Deep Purple were heralded as America's top album selling act.

This in fact was for sales in the year of 1973 and achieving their victory they had beaten out acts like Neil Diamond, Elvis Presley, David Bowie and Elton John.

Purple, in their mark three version, continued much as before, touring and recording, through to June, 1975. Then a real bombshell was dropped. Ritchie Blackmore announced that he had quit the band.

Blackmore had considered quitting the band six months previously. Instead he set to work on what was originally mooted as a solo album. The band he assembled round himself consisted of the remnants of a New York based outfit called Elf — lining-up as Ronnie James Dio (vocals), Gary Driscoll (drums), Micky LeeSoule (keyboards) and Craig Gruber (bass). Their first album was called "Rainbow", as was the band.

Blackmore's replacement was a young American called Tommy Bolin. Just 23 years old he'd been in the James Gang and was an experienced session guitarist playing with such notables as Billy Cobham and Alphonse Mouzon.

However, despite being recommended to Purple by Blackmore, Bolin seemed an odd choice. He had never seen the band perform, nor had he heard any of their albums.

Purple released their first album with Bolin in October 1975 — titled *Come Taste The Band*. It wasn't a particularly strong offering and showed indications of a lack of cohesion and motivation in the band. In July 1976 Deep Purple decided to call it a day. They had achieved an enormous amount, both musically and financially, but the stiff recording and touring schedules had finally taken their toll.

Within a month Jon Lord and Ian Paice had formed the foundations for a new band — called Paice, Ashton, Lord. The Ashton was Tony Ashton (keyboard player), previously with Ashton, Gardner and Dyke, bass guitarist Paul Martinez, previously with Stretch and guitarist Bernie Marsden whose extensive career included stints with Babe Ruth and Wild Turkey.

Glen Hughes and David Coverdale went off to pursue separate solo careers while Tommy Bolin returned to the States to sort out his own future. Bolin died some months later, while Hughes has done little of note.

Paice, Ashton, Lord recorded just one album, *Malice In Wonderland*, and folded within a year. Coverdale recorded a brace of solo albums — *Whitesnake* and *Northwind* before deciding, in his own words, that rock and roll can't be written "in your living room".

So he set about forming a band, called Whitesnake. The first recruit was Mickey Moody, who had co-written some of Coverdale's solo outings. He's also been guitarist with Juicy Lucy, among others. Next was the aforementioned Bernie Marsden, followed by former Colosseum II and National Health bass guitarist Neil Murray. Drummer David Dowle completed the line-up. That line-up recorded the *Trouble* album, in the middle of which Jon Lord joined on keyboards. David Dowle subsequently left to be replaced by Ian Paice — thus reuniting the three former Purple musicians.

Whitesnake has since emerged as a major band and currently stands as the premier Purple shoot-shoot — that's at the end of 1980.

However, between his departure from Purple and today Ritchie Blackmore has probably achieved more success with his various Rainbow blow-ups. He's been through plenty of sidemen during his time, including bass guitarist Roger Glover, but the essential charisma and talent of Blackmore has meant he has retained an enormous following.

During the autumn of 1980 Blackmore split the most successful of the Rainbow line-ups at the time of going to press has yet to announce his future. However in the company of drummer Cozy Powell and singer Graham Bonnet Blackmore

JON BONHAM, LED ZEPPELIN

achieved enormous success throughout the world.

Blackmore's albums — *Rainbow Rising*, *Rainbow*, *On Stage*, *Long Live Rock And Roll*, *Down To Earth* — have all achieved remarkably strong sales figures. As a further indication of his status Blackmore and his band headlined one of the major outdoor festivals in Britain during 1980, the Monsters Of Rock Festival at Castle Donnington, and pulled out a startlingly powerful performance.

Predicting where Blackmore will go next is like being a race track tipster. But whatever he does it's bound to be successful and interesting.

Ian Gillan has had more of a chequered career. On leaving Purple he took some time off from the music business before returning to action with the Ian Gillan Band album *Child In Time* with Island Records in 1975. He recorded two further albums for the same company — *Clear Air Turbulence* and *Scarabus*.

Gillan shifted to Acrobat Records for the next album *Mr Universe* which re-established him as a British chart artist. The band subsequently shifted to Virgin Records to release *Glory Road*. That line-up was Mick Underwood (drums), John McCoy (bass), Bernie Tormé (guitar) and Colin Towns (keyboards).

The band was simply called Gillan at that stage — possibly as a reference to the fact Gillan himself was, up to the end of 1980, about the only stable factor in the outfit's line-up over the years. Nevertheless it was good to see him back in action with a fine band and producing outstanding music. Gillan looks to be one of heavy metal's stayers — and he is still possessed of one of the most distinctive and powerful voices in the business.

Following the trials, tribulations and ups and downs in the collective careers of Black Sabbath and Deep Purple, it comes as something of a relief to approach Led Zeppelin — one of the most successful bands in the history of rock.

That feeling is tempered by the sad death of drummer John Bonham who died in the autumn of 1980. At the time of writing the other three members of the band — Jimmy Page, Robert Plant and John Paul Jones — had not made clear their intentions for the future. It's to be hoped that this most cultured and varied of bands will continue to bring out the kind of music that has graced the rock and heavy metal world for the last dozen years.

Originall Jimmy Page wanted Terry Reid and B.J. Paul to complete the line-up of the New Yardbirds, with John Paul Jones. But the pair weren't available. So Robert Plant and John Bonham were brought in instead. It was a tough decision for Bonham, though. He was earning a steady £40 a week and he wasn't keen, initially, on taking the risk of joining an untried band.

The band renamed themselves Led Zeppelin and their first move was to fulfil a contractual obligation by recording an album. It took them about 30 hours after which the band split for Scandinavia to complete the old Yardbirds' date sheet.

Britain was apathetic towards the band at first and so their manager, Peter Grant, suggested that concentrating on the American market would be a better move. Grant played an enormous role in the band's establishment and continuing growth to

ROBERT PLANT, LED ZEPPELIN

JIMMY PAGE, LED ZEPPELIN

their present super-superstar status.

The album — simply titled *Led Zeppelin* — was released in February 1969. In April it was in the British charts and by the time it slipped out of the Top Twenty in October it was replaced by *Led Zeppelin II* which was the band's first to reach number one in this country.

In America Zeppelin played just one support tour. That was with Vanilla Fudge in the spring of 1969. Following that it was headline tours all the way with America remaining their main target. Within a year of that first tour they had another six in the States which achieved a two-fold purpose: it made them known in as much of America as possible while simultaneously granting them a mystique and air of elusiveness in their native Britain.

Anyone who suggested that this was either luck or coincidence obviously has no idea of the business acumen of Grant — easily one of the great rock managers in history.

From their start until the present day Zeppelin was more regularly seen in the States than in any other part of the world. Britain was confined to an annual glimpse. At the same time Grant ensured that the band was rationed to an album a year. This was not merely a commercial consideration, however. It allowed Zeppelin time to polish up their recorded material, it gave them breathing space to bring out an excellent album every year without feeling they were under too much pressure to meet contractual recording obligations.

Thus the release of every Zeppelin album became an event and none of the events were ever disappointing, either in terms of the music contained or the commercial success achieved.

The impact of the band's albums in this country was never diluted by the release of singles. Their live performances, similarly, were never pre-empted by appearances on the vacuous 'pop' television programmes, like Top Of The Pops.

In short they were kept exclusive and elusive through their own choice and through the guidance of Peter Grant.

On the musical front the band's third album, simply titled *Led Zeppelin III* showed a slight change in direction for the band. Released in 1970 it revealed that there was very much a quasi-folk, semi-mystic air to their music as well as all out rock and roll assault. The fans took the changes in their stride and gave Zeppelin another number one album.

Heartened by this response Zeppelin came up with what is undoubtedly their finest album ever — *Led Zeppelin IV*. This contained what has become the Zeppelin anthem, "Stairway To Heaven". It also laid down the formula for the majority of Zepp's subsequent material, or at least those songs which were not out and out rock and rollers. "Stairway" is acoustic for much of its length, starting in slow, gentle, subtle fashion. Gradually as it progresses an air of power and menace is introduced until it breaks into full-tilt heavy metal. And then, unlike most of its contemporary compositions it has a denouement — an emphatic quietening and a definite end. The phrase tour de force could well have been invented to describe this song.

Following that album, released in 1971, Led Zeppelin followed a simple classic route into their progression.

They played bigger and bigger venues across the world. The opened up British live performance to an unprecedented extent. In 1975, for example, they did a remarkable five nights at London's Earls Court — the biggest indoor venue available to rock — and attracted sell-out audiences every night, scoring a grand total attendance of around 100,000 people.

The albums followed annually — *Houses Of The Holy*, *Physical Graffiti*, *Presence*, *The Song Remains The Same* and *In Through The Out Door*.

The band formed their own record label, Swan Song, and unlike many other artist-headed companies it continues today with a good artist roster and a sound financial basis. They did a remarkable two days of Knebworth Festival and broke all records for attendance.

Their film, *The Song Remains The Same*, was castigated by the critics and enjoyed by the fans. In short nothing seemed to go wrong at all with the Led Zeppelin story. That is up until the year when, sadly, John Bonham died. Quite where that leaves the remainder of the band, no-one knows. Certainly we have no intention of harping on about Bonham's death, except to say that it brought an end to the first, startling era of a remarkable band. They transcended the confines of heavy metal with ease and yet still remained, at heart, a hard rock band. They knew that and the fans did too. One can only hope 1980 did not mark the end of Zeppelin.

While Black Sabbath, Deep Purple and Led Zeppelin were the three major bands to emerge from the golden age of heavy metal they were by no means on their own.

The pomp-rock end of HM was given a power assited lift in 1968 and 1969 with the formation of Genesis, Yes and Emerson, Lake & Palmer, and the replacement of Syd Barrett in Pink Floyd by Dave Gilmour.

No-one but the deafest would ever describe Yes, Genesis or Floyd as HM bands, although they've had an immense influence on successors, notably Canadian HM maestros Rush.

But ELP is another matter. They were formed by Keith Emerson, of the aforementioned Nice, Carl Palmer from Atomic Rooster, and Greg Lake from King Crimson.

Their formation came as the result of an American tour which King Crimson and Nice did in 1969. Emerson and Lake quit their respective bands and lured Palmer from Atomic Rooster. Initially Palmer was unsure of the move and with Rooster doing well during the subsequent two years he probably spent some sleepless nights wondering whether he'd done the right thing.

However, 1970 saw the release of the album *Emerson, Lake & Palmer* which was dominated by Emerson's pyrotechnic keyboard work and which charted well on both sides of the Atlantic. The band borrowed from classical composers like Bartók and Janacek and established a formula which they did not err from in the subsequent eight years.

Even the most generous of their fans would have to agree that their music at times tended to the pompous and their stage activity was completely unpolluted by restraint in any form.

Nevertheless their style and musical formula worked well for them. Hailed as a supergroup they certainly lived up to that tag in commercial success.

Tarkus came out in 1971 and was marked with a stage show of gargantuan proportions. However it was merely a foretaste of their next album — the monster *Pictures At An Exhibition*. It was based on a work by Russian composer Mussorgsky and established ELP as the major pomp-rock band of all time.

From there ELP went gradually downhill all the way. The albums became either excessive in the extreme — *Trilogy*, *Brain Salad Surgery* — or what merely appeared to be contractual obligation outings — *Welcome Back My Friends To The Show That Never Ends*.

In 1977 ELP gave notice of their imminent disintegration with the release of *Works Volume One*. In fact this double album was really three solo outings by the individual members with only half of one side counting as a group effort.

From that point the band gradually petered out with no-one really sure whether they existed in group format or not for some time. The important thing about them was that they were consummate performers — Emerson remains one of the most brilliant keyboard players to grace rock — who exercised much influence over musicians who were to succeed them. They also had a negative influence — and again this was tied in with their sheer skill.

The band's air of ''serious music to be taken seriously'' was eventually to lead to the punk/new wave backlash and in turn to the New Wave of British Heavy Metal. But that's another story to be related later in this book.

While ELP were being deadly serious and musicianly it's doubtful if anyone would have suggested the same of Uriah Heep. One American critic went so far as to suggest he would commit suicide if the band's first album, *Very 'Eavy, Very 'Umble* were to achieve any commercial success. It did, as a matter of fact, but whether the journalist fulfilled his part of the bargain has never been known.

With the exception of Black Sabbath, Uriah Heep have probably been the most critically detested of the heavy metal bands. But that didn't stop them pursuing a ten year career which saw them earning immense success in Germany, the United States and Britain.

They were formed when guitarist Mick Box, singer David Byron and keyboard player Ken Hensley met up in 1970. Up until 1972 the band was unable to boast a permanent rhythm section until they settled on bass guitarist Gary Thain and drummer Lee Kerslake. They'd previously tried bassists Mark Clark and Paul Newton and percussionists Nigel Olsson, Ian Clarke, Keith Baker and Alan Napier.

It was with the Thain/Kerslake line-up that Heep made their major penetration in 1972. That was also the year that the albums *Demons And Wizards?* and *Magicians Birthday* were released.

It was in the States, and Germany, that Heep were initially accepted but, by 1974, they had achieved major success in Britain too, notably with the release of *Wonderworld*. This success was re-

JOHN PAUL JONES, LED ZEPPELIN

affirmed with *Return To Fantasy* and the release of the *Best Of* compilation.

A totally manic band, Heep made their greatest impact on stage with Mick Box and David Byron behaving like a pair of crazed Mexican bandits and Ken Hensley violating his Hammond.

The band endured many setbacks in its career with the death of Gary Thain and the public sacking of David Byron among them.

This year saw the departure of Kerslake for Ozzy Osbourne's new band and the resignation of Ken Hensley, leaving Box, ex-Spider from Mars Trevor Bolder, Chris Slade and John Sloman in charge of the Heep heritage. What the future of the outfit is remains unknown but it seems less than likely they'll repeat any of their past success.

As we've said before the influence of Jimi Hendrix has been enormous and no more so than in the career of Robin Trower who is easily one of the best HM guitarists around.

Trower started his professional career with an R&B band called the Paramounts in Southend. He moved from there to Procol Harum, of all bands, with whom he remained until 1971.

He formed Jude with singer Frankie Miller, ex-Jethro Tull drummer Clive Bunker, bass guitarist Jimmy Dewar from Stone The Crows. The band was short-lived and Trower was quickly into his next phase — the Robin Trower Group — retaining Dewar (doubling on vocals) and adding Reg Isadore.

That line-up released *Twice Removed From Yesterday* in 1973. Then Isadore left and was replaced by Bill Lordan. This new conglomeration

really cracked it with *Bridge Of Sighs* and *From Earth Below* which established Trower as a major act in the States.

In 1976 Trower brought in Rustee Allen to take over bass allowing Dewar to concentrate on vocals. This line-up brought out *Robin Trower Live!*, the exquisite *Long Misty Days*, *In City Dreams* and *Caravan To Midnight*.

Sadly the majority of Trower's success has been confined to America. In Britain he is generally dismissed as a Hendrix copyist. However, this takes away from his natural and native ability as a guitarist. He is a lyrical player who combines quiet quality with immense force.

From the beginning of the 1970s heavy metal was strengthened with the addition of a wave of new bands. Thin Lizzy led by the irrepressible Phil Lynott breezed in from Ireland, Motorhead emerged — midway through the decade — from the ashes of Hawkwind, Nazareth switched from being a semi-pro bar band to an internationally acclaimed outfit, Queen produced a hybrid of glam and HM, Budgie bashed on in the wilds of Wales and Judas Priest played anywhere and everywhere in a five year rise "to overnight success" — a description which might also be applied to UFO.

Thin Lizzy was formed in 1970 in Dublin by bass guitarist, singer and main composer Phil Lynott and drummer Brian Downey. With them was guitarist Eric Bell. The band established itself well enough in its backyard and then moved to London to try its chances there. A contract with Decca led to three albums and a single — "Whiskey

In The Jar" which was a rock version of an Irish song and charted in Britain. Follow-ups proved unsuccessful though and for a while it looked like Lizzy were to join the ranks of one hit wonders.

However, a move to Phonogram records, the departure of Bell — to be replaced by guitarists Scott Gorham and Brian Robertson — brought a new and more vital Lizzy.

By dint of constant touring, added to astute management and good songs the band enhanced its reputation. Albums like *Night Life*, *Fighting*, *Jailbreak* and *Johnny The Fox* indicated they were a band to be reckoned with.

The major breakthrough, however, came with the release of *Bad Reputation* in 1977. The band broke through on both sides of the Atlantic and remain a major attraction. They reaffirmed their status with the double set *Live And Dangerous*.

They are still prone to personnel problems though. Robertson left the band (twice!), was replaced by Gary Moore who also left and Brian Downey had a leave of absence too.

Nevertheless with the mainspring of Phil Lynott behind them they look assured.

The Lizzies, in true heavy metal style, have already spawned a pair of offshoot bands. The first to be formed was Brian Robertson's Wild Horses, set up in 1978, by the diminutive lead guitarist with the equally diminutive bass guitarist Jimmy Bain, formerly of one of Ritchie Blackmore's Rainbows.

As yet the Horses have achieved little in terms of commercial success — despite being a fine band — and it seems that they have their work cut out to break through.

The other offshoot outfit is Gary Moore's G Force. Moore enjoyed a single hit with "Parisienne Walkways" while he was still a member of Thin Lizzy. And, despite the fact that Phil Lynott's vocals were probably as important in the record's success as Moore's guitar work, it seems to have encouraged him to pursue a solo career yet again.

G-Force, formed in 1980, featured Moore, drummer Mark Nauseef, bass guitarist Tony Newman and singer Willie Dee. They recorded a debut album in the summer of 1980 which seemed to be little more than a vehicle for Moore's guitar work.

While Lizzy have endured no end of personnel changes and ups and downs Nazareth have remained stable, relatively speaking, for a decade and a half. Originally known as the Shadettes in their home town of Dunfermline, Pete Agnew (bass), Dan McCaffery (vocals) and Darrell Sweet (drums) changed their name to Nazareth when they were joined by guitarist Manny Charlton in 1969.

They released their first album, *Nazareth*, in 1971 and a few months later switched from semi-pro to professional band.

The band remained a basic, hard-rocking outfit — distinguished by McCaffery's sandpaper voice and Charlton's blues-orientated guitar — right up until 1979 and the addition of second guitarist Zal Cleminson from the Alex Harvey Band.

It was, at that stage, that the band went decidedly West Coast. However, before that time, they had been responsible for some sterling HM performances — such as "Expect No Mercy", "Hair Of The Dog", "Bad Bad Boy" and "This Flight Tonight".

It was the latter song that helped, more than anything else, to alienate them from Britain. Because of Canada's peculiar rules on radio airplay, and the fact that "This Flight Tonight" was written by Canadian Joni Mitchell, meant that the band enjoyed greater acceptance and recognition in that country than they did in their native Britain.

That, plus the media resistance to hard rock and heavy metal bands in the middle to late Seventies, meant that Nazareth always enjoyed more recognition and better record sales in Canada than Britain. As a result, and only to be expected, the band ignored Britain to a relative degree. They are currently more or less written off here — which is an enormous pity since they have much to offer musically.

If Nazareth paid a little more attention to critical response than they should have done Hawkwind and their offshoot Motorhead should be credited with one major facet — they never gave a goddam what anyone thought about them.

Hawkwind is scarcely of importance to this history *per se* — except for the fact that in 1980 they absorbed drummer Ginger Baker into their ranks and for the fact that they spawned Lemmy, *eminence noire* of the New Wave of British Heavy Metal.

It was Lemmy who was responsible for Hawkwind's breakthrough single "Silver Machine" back in 1972. However, by the time 1975 came round, Lemmy (bass guitar) had left/been kicked out of Hawkwind. He immediately set about forming Motorhead which was essentially to be an example

NAZARETH

of the more basic side of Hawkwind's space-rock.

Motorhead had a faltering start in that Lemmy selected guitarist Larry Wallis and drummer Lucas Fox to assist him. The line-up was ineffective and the band's album for United Artists was not, at the time, released. However, Lemmy bounced back with a new line-up and — three years later — a new recording contract.

The contract was with Bronze Records, with whom Motorhead remain, and the two new members were drummer Phil (Philthy Animal) Taylor and guitarist Fast Eddie Clark.

Before signing up with Bronze the existing Motorhead released an album and single for independent label Chiswick — both were called, with characteristic simplicity, *Motorhead*.

The band has subsequently released the *Overkill*, *Bomber* and *Ace Of Spades* albums. And their live appearances have grown bigger and more over the top. Somehow, despite no great ability nor anything which separates them out from other thrash and bash bands, Motorhead have taken an air of being a heavy metal band *par excellence*. Perhaps it is simply their credo of playing harder, heavier, louder and faster than anyone else which has turned the trick.

While Motorhead proved a pleasant surprise to HM fans — maintaining their persona of loud and loutish lunatics to the bitter end — Queen didn't take too long to prove a bitter disappointment.

Thus, having established that, this book proposes to outline their progress only up until the release of the infamously successful single

MOTORHEAD

PHIL LYNOTT

"Bohemian Rhapsody" — which was the final straw in a process of changing the imaginative HM exponents to commercial, mainline popsters.

Two former members of Smile — guitarist Brian May and drummer Roger Taylor — teamed with Freddie Mercury (vocals) and John Deacon (bass) to form Queen in 1972. They were touted as a glamrock band in the beginning, a marketing tactic which was nearly the end of them right at the start since glamrock was a dead duck by the early Seventies.

However, the release of their first album *Queen* in 1972 showed that there was a good deal of substance beneath the band's ostensible and ostentatious style. The single "Seven Seas Of Rhye" showed that they were a commercial proposition — a facet amply demonstrated by *Queen II* and the third album *Sheer Heart Attack*.

It was in the latter that Queen reached their pinnacle as a metal band. This was particularly demonstrated by "I'm In Love With My Car", "Brighton Rock" and the ever superb guitarwork of the highly underrated Brian May.

Alas, for the band's HM followers 1975 brought the album *A Night At The Opera* and the single "Bohemian Rhapsody". The band veered into musical flatulence and Freddie Mercury's decadent public persona and that was the end of them, musically speaking. They were still, of course, recording and selling records by the ton at the end of 1980 but they were well out of the HM sphere by then.

Finally, Judas Priest and UFO — who fall between the first wave of British heavy metal and the second. Both bands were formed at the beginning of the Seventies and yet neither really made it in a major fashion before 1978.

And it's only now that both UFO and Priest are enjoying the commercial fruits of their labours over the years.

UFO was formed in 1971 by singer Phil Mogg, bass guitarist Pete Way and drummer Andy Parker. In 1973 the band parted company with its original guitarist and drafted in ex-Scorpions man Michael Schenker. By this stage the band had only recorded one official album — *UFO* — which was a hit in Germany and Japan but did little elsewhere.

In 1974 the band signed up with Chrysalis Records, where they still remain, and produced a series of ever better albums starting with *Phenomenon* and proceeding through *Force It, No Heavy Petting, Lights Out, Obsession, Strangers In The Night* and *No Place To Run*.

During that period they lost Schenker to the odd Moony sect, regained him with no explanation from the guitarist, and then lost him again. He was replaced temporarily and then permanently by former Lone Star guitarist Paul Chapman.

For Judas Priest it was close on half a decade before they began to attract national attention. Founded by singer Rob Halford, guitarist K.K. Downing and bass player Ian Hill, the band had to wait for a surprise live success at Reading Festival before they were noticed.

It was probably the fact that former Purple bass guitarist Roger Glover recorded their third album *Sin After Sin* their helped them along the road.

Priest, like UFO, have simply come up with better and better albums — *Stained Glass, Killing Machine, Unleashed In the East, British Steel* — and worked hard and heavy in halls, clubs and stadia all over the world.

It's fitting that this section of the book ends with Priest and UFO for they bridge an important gap between the old wave and the new wave of HM in Britain — not only chronologically but also stylistically and from the point of view of approach to the fans.

Chronologically goes without saying for it is by now self-evident that the first wave of HM faded away from national prominence in 1975.

Stylistically the pair maintain the grandiose outlines of the old bands and yet capture the frenetic amphetamine-charged pace of the New Wave of HM.

Their approach to the fans and to the basic fact of playing live is an intriguing subject however. It was because the old bands went over the top in choosing to record infrequently and tour occasionally that helped to alienate them from such a large sector of the British public.

This led to the punk/new wave backlash — sponsored by those who felt that you didn't have to go to Earls Court once a year to hear music. It could be made in any place at any time.

This in turn led to the rise of the second wave of British HM. But, in the meantime, there were hard-working and stylish bands like Priest and UFO who kept the HM flag waving and the torch burning. They played everywhere at any time and they have reaped the results today. It's no wonder the're doing as well as they are now.

UFO

RORY GALLAGHER

RUNNING WITH THE DEVIL. USA '66-'80

There can be little doubt that the United States has played a considerably central role in the provision of heavy metal entertainment throughout the past 15 years or so. Indeed it was in America that the actual phrase 'Heavy Metal' was first used in an artistic sense (by William Burroughs) and subsequently translated into a contemporary musical setting (by Sandy Pearlman). However, the fact remains that true HM has and probably never will really exist in the States. Why? Well taking as a working definition the whole genre as revolving around fiery, crackling guitar riffs overladen with raw, aggressive noise-toy volume, then it soon becomes patently obvious that the US doesn't ever produce such artisans. Rather they go in for a more refined approach, marrying together the basics of HM with a subtler image and outlook — in short hard-rock or, if you prefer, heavy rock. The difference may seem pedantic, yet has ensured that whilst the likes of Led Zeppelin found comparatively little difficulty in opening up the Americas to their sound and visions, the likes of Black Sabbath (at least in their earlier days) never made a significant impact on the millions of teen-agers who have taken the music to their hearts and wallets.

So where did it all start, US-wise? Like most explosions of fashion within rock 'n' roll, the Americans were largely influenced by the British scene and its variations of the HM front. Indeed, for the country that initiated the embryonic development of rock 'n' roll in the first place by fusing together white country & western with the black blues via such legends as Bill Haley and Elvis Presley, to actually be privy to changes in atmosphere from across the Atlantic is certainly a trifle odd at first, without attempting a detailed analysis, suffice it to say that America has for some time now been about two years or so behind the UK in acknowledging and accepting trends in music and are clearly equally loathe to give up a genre once it is established. The very first heavy rock (as we should denote US bands of this ilk) group to emerge from the playing fields of Harvard (metaphorically speaking, of course) is a matter for historical conjecture. Some would point the finger at Grand Funk Railroad, who, despite the soulful nature of their monicker, dealt, during the latter part of the Sixties, out a sound so loud that even to this day, people still talk of bleeding ears at their massive concerts. Other names that crop up in the quest for the original American heavy rock outfit include Jimi Hendrix who, although born in the States, really made his major impact across the Atlantic in the UK (as already dealt with in the chapter on the rise of British metal), Iron Butterfly, the first band of this ilk to actually earn platinum album status via the mysteriously-named *In A Gadda Da-Vida* during the last couple of years of the Sixties and even Bob Dylan, whose earlier songs were certainly, in content at least, in phase with what was to follow on the traditional heavy rock scene.

However, to the minds of many, that accolade of the US heavies' ancestral beginners belongs to the Byrds, indeed the first group to be actually termed 'heavy metal'. Sure, this bunch of five American musicians dealt primarily in the production of pop melodies following in the wake of the Beatles, Who and Rolling Stones, but there can be

little doubt that their guitar-orientated treatment of Dylan's "Mr Tambourine Man" incorporated many of the tricks of the trade that have become familiar patterns within modern American rock. Other numbers such as "Eight Miles High" again showed the way forward and if at the time those musicians who did tread the same path as the Byrds ended up failing to recognise their exploratory tendencies then this can simply be put down to the fact that neither the time nor the people were ready or willing to accept a heavier form of music into everyday life.

Naturally, of course, the spread of flower-power and the entire hippy outlook to America played its part in the sowing of the heavy rock seeds, but again much of the contemporary scene inside the US was geared up towards the less complex musical side of things and although festivals like Woodstock did figure significantly in the moulding of public tastes, they nonetheless, never really altered American music in the way that Cream, Hendrix, Hawkwind and the Pink Floyd were doing over in Britain. Why? Perhaps, it was down to the sheer size of the States. Cracking that vast market was to give oneself over to the Americas for a period of years and many musicians didn't have either the time or the inclination to make their homes permanently away from European climates and influences.

All this, in many ways, does go against the history books as they painted the rise of rock in the States. Yet a cursory glance at the bands around during the 1967-69 era and a listen to their material does prove that, in the final analysis, US heavy

LYNYRD SKYNYRD

machinery just wasn't up to British standards.

Indeed, even when the likes of Zeppelin and Purple at last broke through into the wild west d beyond, taking their powerhouse brand of m_ ti-decibel warfare with 'em and inspiring mass hysteria at concerts across both the East and West coasts, the search on that enormous continent for home-grown equivalents didn't in the main throw up many possibilities. Too great a proportion of those around at the time were merely clones of their UK heroes, trying to copy their sound and not really doing any-thing about adapting it for American consumption. And, inevitably, youngsters in the US would only turn to this form of music in the bars and clubs when, and only when, they had nowhere to turn for better UK originals.

The band who started the revolution against this and really showed that Americans could do what the British did, only better (in some ways, at least) were a four-piece by the name of Montrose. In 1973, they put out their debut album on Warner Brothers and took the heavy world by storm. What they had done was to take the raw English riffs of the big names and smooth them out sufficiently to lose the hard blues core and replace it with a more up-to-date commercial angle. Not the first to try this by any means, Montrose did however succeed in their efforts and finally opened the doors to US bands of the genre. Numbers such as "Rock The Nation", "Bad Motor Scooter" and, more than anything else, "Space Station Number Five", captured the public's imagination on both sides of the Atlantic and to this day remain bona fide classics. Sadly, though, the band could never again equal (let alone surpass) this massive achievement and subsequent releases like "Paper Money" were just pale imitations. But from within the ranks of this great outfit has come one of today's most exciting heavy rock ex-ponents — Sammy "Red Devil" Hagar. A fitness fanatic and a veritable fiend on stage, Hagar is a man who has in many ways dominated the American scene in recent years, via albums such as *Red*, *Nine On A Ten Scale*, *All Night Long* (a blistering live offering) and *Street Machine*. The man is one of those who turned to rock 'n' roll because of hardship and has certainly made it work on his behalf, earning him a reputation that has spread in recent years throughout the rockin' world. What he represents is the triumph of the individual against all the odds, a story-line Americans love to hear; he is a real hero and his live outpourings of high-volume rhythmic noise is typical of a certain small breed of larger-than-life charismatic figures who, more than anyone else on the US scene come closest to crossing over into British HM. Another member of this union of uncompromising muthas is Ted Nugent. A former member of a cult band by the name of the Amboy Dukes, nutty Nugent has made his name by proclaiming the value and vitality of volume for its own sake. He actively encourages insanity at concerts and once enunciated that "if it's too loud you're too old". Nugent's music, like that of Hagar, clearly follows the line that when played to its limit, decibelisation can be THE MOST invigorating form of music on the scene. Though some of the most spectacular albums to come out of America during the past few years, Nugent has claimed a special position for himself in the hearts and minds of HR fans everywhere. Even to this day, *Ted Nugent*, *Free For All* and *Double Live Gonzo* remain hot stuff in anyone's language.

Away from the cult of the individual, America has also thrown up over the years an enormous quantity of bands who've made significant world-wide impact. Take Kiss, for instance, can there be much doubt that this bunch of make-up 'n' mayhem inducers could only have been conceived in America? Coming on-stage in the most outrageous costumes and possessing some of the finest special effects man could invent, Kiss, since their advent under the astute guidance of manager Bill Aucoine in the mid-seventies, have transformed their shows more into carnivals than concerts, allowing their fans (many of whom are in their early teens and younger!) to live out comic-strip fantasies, dressing up in the same way as their heroes and being taken a journey into a world inhabited by the unbelievable and the astonishing. You don't go to a Kiss gig to witness the music as much as to become enthralled by the ex-perience. Indeed, much of their vinyl offerings have been on the poor side and following in the over-the-top traditions of Busby Berkely, Cecil B deMille and, most importantly of all, Walt Disney, this band have turned heavy rock into a circus format anyone can enjoy. Proof of just how phenomenally success-ful this outlook has been comes from the fact that they are currently the fifth largest corporation in America and marketable goods from lawnmowers to pin-ball machines are sold in their thousands not to mention two comic-books being put together in their honour (Kiss as superheroes on a par with Spiderman, Superman and, most obviously, the Fantastic Four) and a film entitled *Kiss Meet The Phantom Of The Park*. More than that the whole Kiss style is enhanced by their determination never to be photographed without their make-up, once more underlining a mystique value to their image.

Image, in fact, is at the core of so much on the heavy rock side of American music and, aside from Kiss, so many bands have attempted to build repu-tations on the basis of developing spectacular stage-shows although none has made it in the way Aucoine's proteges have. Take Angel for instance, a five-piece delving into the world of sexual hints and innuendos, they originally came to the fore after being spotted by Gene Simmonds (of Kiss) who was sufficiently impressed with what he saw to recom-mend them to his own label, Casablanca, and a deal ensued. The concept of Angel, as the name suggests, is based around the power of white. Everything from the mike stands to their clothing was adorned with the colour of purity, which is more than can be said for their act, a pouting, strutting derivative of the bi-sexual glam-rock era with much that although heavy leans very much into the sphere of pop. The failures of albums like *On Earth As It Is In Heaven*, *Helluva*

Band and *Sinful*, seem to have persuaded them to change their direction and outlook but, once again the force of the visual side of American rock comes to the fore.

Elsewhere, Aerosmith have certainly suffered from the fact that their music just hasn't spread outside of the American borders and to a great extent this can be put down to a lack of direct freshness about the stuff they have put out. It's arguable that the band only came onto the scene in a big way because of a gap due to the long-term absence of the British stars and the public therefore looking around for a suitable soundalike to replace them. Throw in vocalist Steve Tyler's not inconsiderable resemblance to Mick Jagger and a set of albums with little or no easily identifiable individuality(as opposed to innovation) and you have the makings of the reasons why the US has accepted them whereas elsewhere they've been ignored. However, the music on albums like *Rocks*, *Toys In The Attic* and *Night In The Ruts* has proved too powerfully compelling and even the loss of guitarist Joe Perry, a leading light in the 'Smith passage to fame, hasn't altogether extinguished their future hopes.

The US, though, is filled to capacity with a whole range of outfits who are big at home yet mean little anywhere else. Take REO Speedwagon; ever since this Illinois five-piece launched their vinyl career in 1971 with *REO Speedwagon*, they have enjoyed steadily increasing success in the States with a sound that combines sweet melodies with a rock 'n' raunch approach to riffing. Yet as the likes of "Ridin' The Storm Out", "REO", "You Can Tune A Piano, But You Can't Tuna Fish" and "Nine Lives" have come, and gone from the US charts, the band are virtually no more than a cult band with a small group of diehard fanatics in the UK and haven't really broken out of their home market. Why, then, does this sort of thing happen? Here we must turn to the whole arrangement of heavy rock in the USA. As has already been indicated, blitzing HM has never been the Americans' bag, rather they have tended to disperse their resources into a number of different directions at once, preserving the sound of HR yet also giving it an indelible stamp of US ownership.

Take, for instance, AOR. Adult-Orientated Rock is a title that basically describes the use of heavy rock rhythms in the core of a commercially airplayable sound, the sort of thing you can listen to on a freeway without running the risk of driving your car into the nearest lay-by as you headbang into a frenzy. Foreigner are a prime example of just how such a sound can be achieved. Formed in '77 by various members of British groups like Spooky Tooth and King Crimson plus US musicians also in-tune with what was happening, they spent many weeks in the studio culling together a cohesive approach that would not only crack the commercial end of the US market wide open but would also ensure that heavy rock freaks across the nation would get off on their sounds. The result was *Foreigner*, a 10-track album with clearly defined criteria and a sense of production enhancement and embellishment that quickly gave them hit singles with "Cold As Ice" and "Feels Like The First Time" and meant that, finally, many of the band's members were tasting success for in the words of the song "the very first time". Journey, too, after the release of four totally hybrid complex albums in the form of such as *Into The Future* that, although highly impressive from a musical viewpoint, never made any sort of impact on the charts and didn't shift sufficient product. So guitarist Neal Schon, a childhood phenomenon who once played with Santana and was the guiding light behind the entire group, opted for a more obviously commercial angle on their 1978 effort *Infinity* and success was achieved at last. There are countless others who have compromised their heavy duty appeal in order to gain more national recognition and in all honesty it has given rise to a particular US brand of HR, something that, for years, was virtually non-existent.

But AOR is just one form of US-rock that has grown up over the past few years. Another is pomp-rock. Back in the early seventies, bands such as Uriah Heep, Yes, Genesis, and inevitably Deep Purple were beginning to experiment with the addition of classically-inspired sequences in their music, each according to a different strategy. The impact these outfits had on the States was such that as with Zeppelin, their music was taken on-board the American dream and slowly converted into a more acceptable form — POMP. What that meant was various bands attempting to introduce vocal harmonies, more immediate melodies and less aggression into the music, affording it a much more American sound. Among the first to succeed were Kansas, a band with a six-man line-up who aside from 'regular' instruments such as drums, guitars and keyboards also gave rise to the use of violins in a rock setting. Their style was moulded over a period of four albums until with *Leftoverture* in 1976, they at last found a formula which worked, combining familiar patterns of mature musicianship within titles such as "Opus Insert" and "Magnum Opus" yet also providing themselves with distinguishable melody lines that made numbers like "Carry On Wayward Son" successful singles. The band's recognition was soon followed by others and the trend was set. Of course in such a short space attempting to document all of those members of a particular genre is a task well-nigh impossible to achieve, so let's content ourselves with a brief look at just a couple of central pomp-rockers. Styx, for instance, came on the scene in 1971 and at first were signed, strangely enough, to a small Chicago-based label by the name of Wooden Nickel, releasing such LPs as *Styx One*, *Styx Two*, *The Serpent Is Rising* and *Man Of Miracles*, even earning a minor hit with a number by the name of "Lady" before in 1975 hitching their wagon to A&M. Since then, they've gone from strength-to-strength and five albums have entered the charts as they've at last established a strong identity for themselves and earned the admiration of many thousands

But if Styx and Kansas remain central to the immediate past then the band who could be equally important in the future in rejuvenating the pomp-

rock scene is an LA outfit by the name of Rise. Signed to a small label by the title of Mystic in California, the band put out a single coupling up ''Visions'' and ''Twitch City'' early in 1980 that showed a distinct trend back towards hardened rhythmic foundations than has been witnessed in recent pomp releases and they are living proof that this particular aspect of American rock is far from dead.

Way down in the Southern States, you'll come across a true red-necked, ass-kickin' sound that's as American as Jack Daniels and equally as potent — Southern boogie it's called and it has certainly given the world some mean, spitting bands in recent years. Most famous of 'em all are, naturally, Lynyrd Skynyrd who established themselves as one of the great groups of the seventies with a consistent line in firm, powerful music. Originally known as the One Percent, they grew out of their native Jacksonville during the early Seventies, spreading the word wherever they roamed. To this day, numbers such as ''Freebird'', ''Sweet Home Alabama'' etc are still unbeatable classics in their own right. The destruction of the band in '77 when a plane crash killed vocalist Ronnie Van Zant and guitarist Steve Gaines plus backing vocalist Cassie Gaines has left a void yet to be successfully filled, although the likes of Blackfoot, Molly Hatchet, 38 Special (featuring Donnie Van Zant, Ronnie's younger brother) have certainly gone a long way towards offsetting their loss. Out of the same stable, too, came the Allman Brothers Band whose classic cut was an instrumental by the title of ''Jessica'' and a member of which,

guitarist Duane Allman, played on the legendary Derek & The Dominoes song ''Layla''.

But even trying to superficially document the heavy rock scene in a country so vast and varied as America is practically out of the question and in the short space allotted so far, there hasn't been any mention of Blue Oyster Cult or their Svengali Sandy Pearlman, the multi-layered sound that has become the hallmark of Boston, the technically irreproachable Toto and a huge array of other worthies. But it's to the future in the Eighties that one must really look because that is where history is already being made; a new, quite different set of criteria is now in operation and the sounds of tomorrow are starting to blend together.

One outfit who are decidedly operating on a new level are a four-piece by the name of Van Halen. It was in 1977, almost exactly four years after that classic Montrose debut, that the sounds of a bright, fresh and clearly phenomenal talent hit the racks in the form of Van Halen, the debut effort from a group of hopefuls led by the Dutch-descended brothers Eddie (guitar) and Alex (drums) Van Halen and featuring the wiles of one of America's young breed of rock 'n' roll tigers David Lee Roth (vocals) and Michael Anthony (bass). This album caught the attentions of everyone with it's swaggering, confident use of established riff patterns and proved that although there may not be anything new under the sun, nonetheless a fresh approach was possible. Originals like ''Ain't Talking About Love'', ''Running With The Devil'' and ''Icecream Man'' mingled impressively with an astonishing version of the

KANSAS

'SAMMY HAGAR

EDWARD VAN HALEN

Kink's classic "You Really Got Me", arguably the very first metal song from way back in 1965. It was this album, coming as it did just as punk started to grip the UK, which proved heavy rock was far from dead and since then it has inspired others who began to pick up a little speed with their playing not all that far removed from the perpetrators of the new wave of British heavy metal. Bands such as New York's Riot and quintet Legs Diamond (named after a 1930s gangster) have begun to take up the challenge of Van Halen and a future for this type of approach seems assured.

However, the most exciting development to have occurred in the history of US heavy rock during the last five years is still in its infancy — METAL/POP. It was Cheap Trick who set the ball rolling down this path with albums such as *Heaven Tonight*, *Dream Police* and *In Colour*, transforming the licks and riffs of the likes of Aerosmith and AC/DC into more commercially viable formats by using them to beef up what were, when it is all said and done, pop songs of the variety one would expect to hear from the likes of the Move, ELO or the Beatles. That this worked can be attested by the success of such numbers as "I Want You To Want Me" and Cheap Trick, a staggering mixture of zany humour and clean-cut looks, heavy power and sensitive melodies, certainly seemed to be thriving on their new-found guru role. But over the period towards the end of the Seventies and the start of the Eighties, a number of new, vibrant outfits began to challenge their supremacy in this field, among them a considerable proportion with female vocalists. For a kick-off out of Los Angeles came 1994, headed by the winsome Karen Lawrence and over just two albums in *1994* and *Please Stand By*, they thundered through songs of the undeniable calibre of "Our Time Will Come" and "Radio Zone". Sadly the fates have dealt them a bum hand and the band split up not long after their second album appeared on A&M. From New York come Laurie & The Sighs, a quintet fronted by Laurie Beechman and again with a vivacious line in hard melodies as is proven by their one and, to date, only release in the album *Laurie & The Sighs* on Atlantic; Spider are a sextet boasting two females in vocalist Amanda Blue and Holly Knight on keyboards. Signed to Mike Chapman's label Dreamland, they, too, have just one LP out so far in *Spider*, which follows a distinct pattern within the sphere of metal/pop and does it extremely well. Also on this label is Shandi, a female virtuoso who is rather similar to an American Kate Bush with decidedly heavy leanings. But the most interesting band in this whole genre are LA's Storm. Now signed with Capitol, this band are fronted by piledriving powerhouse voice owned by Jeanette Chase and have impressively moulded together influences from the likes of ELO, Queen, Abba, Led Zeppelin and serve the whole thing up within a distinctive over-the-top framework. On vinyl, their only release to date is one album from their previous label, MCA, simply entitled *Storm*.

This, then, is the future, one laden with goodies and possibilities and if what has gone before in this chapter seems a trifle sketchy then remember that what we have tried to do is give a taste of myriad different sounds around on a continent with far more talented and deserving bands than could be handled by even this book.

So far in a chapter supposedly devoted to the workings of the US and Canadian markets for heavy rock, the entire emphasis has been on the former. But it is to the Canadian scene that we must now turn our attentions. It has often been said, in all seriousness that the Canadians are lucky enough to have more heavy rock bands per capita than any other nation on earth. Yet, perhaps, now is the time to make a slight adjustment to this phrase; the Canucks have more GOOD heavy rock bands per capita than you are likely to find anywhere else on this planet, a striking but nonetheless oft-overlooked fact. For much of the past twenty years or so, Canada has been regarded unfairly as merely a piece of land stuck onto the end of the mighty USA, at least from a musical point of view. Much of this has unfortunately come about because to a great extent those Canadian musicians who have broken through and made names for themselves have inevitably not made a conscious attempt to correct the misinformed impression that they must be Americans. In the sphere of heavy rock, as everywhere else, this is a sad truism. The likes of Bachman-Turner Overdrive and Pat Travers have, it must be said, been making important contributions for some time to the world scene, but in actual terms of putting Canadian HR on the map, there is need to mention the name of one band — RUSH.

In no other country on earth has one outfit played such a cornerstone role in the development of its nation's heavier music. Not in the UK, where the likes of Led Zeppelin, Black Sabbath, Cream, Hendrix and Deep Purple can all claim to have had important roles without any being more immediately vital. Not in the States, where again one could name up to a dozen contributors who have had an impact. Not AC/DC in Australia (how many have followed 'em? Cold Chisel and Angel City plus precious few others). Not the Scorpions in Germany (Accept, Stop, Anyone's Daughter, Grobschnitt, and Epitaph being virtually the only other HR bands from that country and none has made it on the international scene). Not Focus in Holland nor Krokus in Switzerland. Rush when a really definitive history of the entire history of Canadian heavy rock comes to be written will stand out from the crowd because when they gained international acceptance then and only then did others from that country emerge into the limelight.

The rise of Rush happened through continuous hard graft in the clubs of their native Toronto with a three-piece line-up of Geddy Lee (bass/vocals), Alex Lifeson (vocals/guitars) and John Rutsey (drums/vocals). The band were starting to fuse together influences such as Deep Purple, Led Zeppelin and Yes, taking small parts from each of these major UK bands and building them up into a working model that contained fiery, basic riffs yet intricate arrangements. The first signs of just how this worked in practice came in 1974 with the release of *Rush*, their debut effort for Anthem Records in Canada and Mercury over in the UK. Even to this day, numbers such as "Finding My Way" and "Working Man" remain favourites with Rush fans. Soon after this album was released, Rutsey left the band

to be replaced by Neil Peart and the new drummer made an immediate impact, not only on the rhythm section of the band but also on their lyrical content. Peart brought a touch of the mystical poetry approach to the Rush canon, hinting at Bradbury, Yes and Lennon yet in the final analysis, possessing a rich texture all their own.

The first album from the new line-up was *Fly By Night* in 1975, featuring a highly expressive cover illustration by Eraldo Carugati and also boasting the production services of a man who has since become a Rush stalwart and almost the fourth member of the band, Terry Brown, responsible for the re-mixing of *Rush* but from *FBN* onwards involved actively from the recording stage onwards. Aside from memorable shots in the heavy rock vein such as ''Anthem'' and ''Rivendell'', this album also featured what has subsequently become a Rush norm — the epic track, in this case ''By-Tor & The Snow Dog'', lasting for just under nine minutes and split into four parts. It's indeed worth looking at Peart's embryonic style of lyric writing as a pointer to the future:

The Tobes of Hades Lite By Flickering Torchlight,
    The Netherworld Is Gathered In The Glare,
Prince By-Tor Taket Of The Cavern To The
        Northlight,
The Sign Of Eth Is Rising In The Air,
    By-Tor-Knight Of Darkness,
Centurion Of Evil, Devil's Prince.

A year later *Caress Of Steel* came onto the market and once more showed the band to be were improving and growing in confidence through the likes of ''Bastille Day'' (''There's no bread let them eat cake/There's no end to what they'll take/Flaunt the fruits of noble birth/Wash the salt into the earth''), ''Lakeside Park'' (''Midway hawkers calling/Try your luck with me/Merry-go-round wheezing/The same old melody''), and ''The Fountain'' (''Look the mist is rising/And sun is peeking through /See, the steps grow lighter/As I reach the final few'').

But the real breakthrough in international terms came in 1976 with *2112*, with the title track, taking up the entire content of side one, dominating the album. Split into seven parts, this took its inspiration from a '30s right-wing American writer by the name of Ayn Rand and contained some of the most powerful combinations and lyrics yet put in harness by the band:

We are the priests of the Temples of Syrinx,
    Our great computers fill the hallowed halls,
We are the priests of the Temples of Syrinx,
    And the gifts of life are held within our walls.

The release of this album created a tremendous controversial storm not only because of the content of the title track but also because of its avowed right-wing influences. Many people began to see the band, unfairly, as fascist sympathisers and articles on this subject dominated the press when the band came to the UK during May/June of 1977, a tour climaxing at the Odeon Hammersmith in London on the 4th June, featuring apart from classics of the

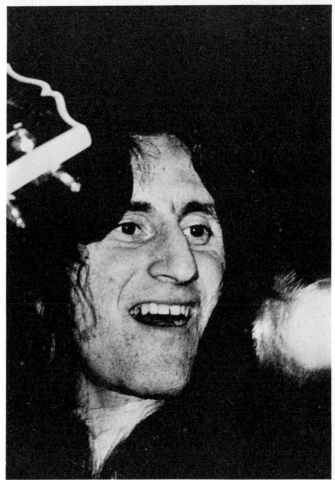

RUSH

calibre of ''Bastille Day'', ''Anthem'' and ''Something For Nothing'' newer numbers such as ''Xanadu'' and ''Cygnus X-I'', both of which appeared on *A Farewell To Kings*, put out during 1977 and from which ''Closer To The Heart'' (''And the men who hold high places/Must be the ones who start/To mould a new reality/Closer to the heart'') was a surprise hit single. This was also the album that introduced synthesiser work into the sphere of Rush music via Lee's use of the mini Moog and the incorporation of the bass pedal synthesiser by both Lee and Lifeson.

By '78, and the release of *Hemispheres*, the band were major heavy rock hearoes all over the world, and, slowly the opening of the way forward for other Canadian outfits began to happen. Supporting Rush on the UK part of the ''Hemispheres tour'' were a four-piece by the name of Max Webster, also from Toronto, whose sound was slightly on the wacky side but perfectly complemented the Rush complexity of mood. Back home in Canada another trio, was beginning to make its presence felt. The band in question were Triumph, lining up as Rich Emmett (guitar/vocals), Mike Levine (bass/vocals) and Gil More (drums/vocals). Having fought on the small circuit for many years, the band finally achieved international interest with the release on RCA of a compilation album by the title of *Rock & Roll Machine* containing tracks from two previously-issued affairs in ''Triumph'' and ''Rock & Roll Machine'' itself. With a sound not unlike that of Rush, the band soon equalled the latter's home appeal, drawing enormous crowds wherever they went and the release of *Just A Game*

in 1979 finally put them into the big league, especially in the US. 1980 has seen the band's fourth album crack the American Top 30 and the British Top 60 charts and also major tours for them with the likes of UFO, Ian Hunter and Toto in the US plus their first ever UK headlining dates.

Remaining in Toronto, Saga have during the course of 1980 suddenly emerged into the arena playing rock with an element of sci-fi culture running right through it. A five-piece with considerable keyboards clout they now have three albums available, each relating the on-going story of a futuristic civilisation on the planet earth and combining together sophisticated heavy music with plots straight out of the '30s era of pulp sci-fi as practiced by the likes of E E Smith, Edgar Rice Burroughs and many others.

Frank Marino & Mahogany Rush have been around for something like a decade now, without ever really making the jump from big to BIG but have consistently delivered a highly aggressive yet somewhat polished sound based around the guitarist's obsession with Jimi Hendrix; at one time he actually claimed to have been imbued with the spirit of Hendrix! Albums such as *World Anthem*, *Tales From The Unexpected* and *What's Next* clearly indicate his class and direction and they are but one of a number of bands who have been around on the scene for some time now. April Wine, for instance, have released some 11 albums over a period of nearly a decade, yet over here are known solely as a band with just two releases on Capitol, *viz*, *Harder . . . Faster* plus *First Glance* and one four-date tour back in February of 1980. Myles Goodwin, vocalist / guitarist with the melodic April Wine, is also known by followers as the guy who produced a couple of albums from yet another Canadian outfit in Teaze and then there's six-piece metal/popsters (or as they prefer to be known ''rock 'n' wavers'') Toronto, born out of the shambles of Rose and Lady and with one album on A&M to their credit in *Lookin' For Trouble*. So it goes on with the likes of Lynx, Myofist (signed up to A&M and with two albums around, the second of which, *Hot Spikes*, is a late '80 release), Jenson Interceptor, Reckless (formerly known as Harlow and managed by the same company that handles Saga; they're on the EMI lable with an album due in early '81), Red Rider (one Capitol album), Heart (a hugely successful six-piece, featuring sisters Nancy and Anne Wilson with a sound more to the AOR side of heavy rock and to be found on the Epic label), Zon (originally on Epic for whom they recorded two highly interesting, not to mention innovative, albums in *Astral Projector* and *Back Down To Earth* and now on the Falcon label in New York) and countless others stretching across the entire spectrum of heavy rock.

Naturally as you will have already found out for yourself, this particular chapter is by no means a definitive exposé on the in-depth history of the development or, indeed, future of heavy rock in the US and Canada but rather has tried to bring to your attention a few key bands and incidents that, hopefully, will have whetted your appetite sufficiently to make hunting down albums by the mentioned artistes well worthwhile. Perhaps, therefore, it

will be of use for a list of possibly relevant and representative albums to be annotated at the end of this part of the book. Below, therefore, we present a selection of titles worth watching out for. This is by no means a list of the greatest albums of all time from USA/Canuck bands but a sample of an enormous population:

''MONTROSE'' — Montrose (WEA)
''VAN HALEN'' — Van Halen (WEA)
''ALIVE TWO'' — Kiss (Casablanca)
''LEFTOVERTURE'' — Kansas (CBS)
''2112'' — Rush (Mercury)
''STORM'' — Storm (MCA)
''1994'' — 1994 (A&M)
''NOTHIN' FANCY'' — Lynyrd Skynyrd (MCA)
''PROGRESSIONS OF POWER'' — Triumph (RCA)
''KILLERWATTS'' — Compilation featuring Blue Oyster Cult, Boston, Molly Hatchet, Mahogany Rush, Aerosmith (Epic)
''LOOKIN' FOR TROUBLE'' — Toronto (A&M)
''SILENT KNIGHT'' — Saga (Polydor)
''PIECES OF EIGHT'' — Styx (A&M)
'LIVE AT THE BUDOKAN' — Cheap Trick (Epic)
''FOREIGNER'' — Foreigner (Atlantic)
''TOMCATTIN'' — Blackfood (WEA)
''REO'' — REO Speedwagon (Epic)

DAVID LEE ROTH

METAL RENDEZVOUS. EUROPE '66-'80

Although hard rock and heavy metal are dominated by the Anglo-American axis it's fair to say that the music is international in character and appeal. That's more true now in the Eighties than ever before.

The majority of "Western" countries are receptive to hard rock in one way or another — but few, with the obvious exceptions of Britain, the United States and Canada, have been responsible for spawning hard rock bands of international stature.

Japan, to illustrate a point, is a massive market for heavy metal. Many artists, most notably Ian Gillan in recent years, have recorded albums specifically for Japan in order to meet that country's seemingly insatiable appetite for heavy metal.

However, the country has yet to come with a major HM band of its own which stands up on the international front. The nearest example was probably the Sadistic Mika Band — back in the middle Seventies — but they were not a big international success, nor were they as heavy as most American or British exponents.

Europe and Australia are by no means as arid as Japan in terms of coming up with their own bands — but at the same time they've not been as productive as the States, Canada or Britain.

However, both Europe and Australia both can boast some major acts and the possibility of more and more coming through looks strong.

Australia's biggest and best known band is obviously AC/DC who, by the end of the Seventies, had transformed themselves within five years from a bunch of hopefuls making their first appearances outside their native land to an internationally acclaimed name outfit.

Formed in Australia back at the beginning of the Seventies, the band originally consisted of Bon Scott (vocals), Angus Young (guitar), Cliff Williams (bass), Malcolm Young (guitar) and Phil Rudd (drums). AC/DC, as the name might indicate, were very much of an outrage band in the same sense as Alice Cooper — hence their much-touted boozing exploits and curious persona of Angus Young as an oversized guitar-toting schoolboy.

AC/DC made their first appearances in the UK in 1976 and made an immediate hit. Their albums from *High Voltage* to *Highway To Hell* were a natural progression from high speed boogie and rock to out and out heavy metal. By dint of hard-touring throughout Europe and the States they established themselves as a top outfit.

In 1980, however, they suffered a major blow with the death of singer Bon Scott through over drinking. However, they bounced back with remarkable ease — and some might say glorious bad taste — with the album *Back In Black*.

They replaced Scott with the equally raucous Brian Johnson, who was previously lead singer with over the top pop band Geordie — who had dabbled on the fringes of heavy metal in the early and middle Seventies.

The only other Australian heavy metal band to take a serious tilt at the international market is Angel City who ventured into the European scene at the beginning of 1980. The band boasted an active lead singer in Doc Neeson and a pair of talented

AD/DC

guitar playing brothers — Rick and John Brewster. Their first album, *Angel City*, proved to be a rough and raucous outing which was a little primitive but augured well for the future.

And that's about it as far as Antipodean bands on the international scene is concerned. The main problem for Australian acts is the cost they would have to bear to launch into a fully fledged tour of Europe and the States. The market is already well served with local acts so the prospect of funding such a tour must seem prohibitive to record companies or managements.

In Europe the main problem appears to have been a certain degree of indifference towards hard rock music. Most countries can be written off without any problem — with the major exception of Germany which is proving to be a fertile area for heavy metal.

But first, the others. France has but one hard rock band worthy of note — Shakin' Street, headed by the lead singer and trainee sex object Fabienne Shine. It was she who formed the band in Paris back in 1975. The band have made a brace of albums — *Vampire Rock* and *Shakin' Street*. They began to make an impact internationally in 1980 when they recruited guitarist Ross The Boss from the Dictators and were taken over for management by Sandy Pearlman, who was instrumental in the formation of Blue Oyster Cult and who also took on Black Sabbath in 1980.

Shakin' Street — which was more of a United Nations microcosm than purely a French band, boasting a Bulgarian, a Frenchman of Russian extraction, and Fabienne herself who has Algerian and Italian influences in her background — toured Europe and the States during 1980 and seemed to have laid the foundations for progress in the future.

Switzerland was the unlikely home of another European act which began attracting attention worldwide in 1980. The band was Krokus and they were the first exponents of HM ever to emerge from the land of the cuckoo clock.

The band consisted of Chris Von Rohr, Tommy Kiefer, Fernando Von Arb, Freddy Steady and lead singer Marc Storace. Storace joined them only in 1980 in time for their third album *Metal Rendezvous* which was the first to receive a release in Britain and the States. Tours of the UK and the US ensued and Krokus looked likely to progress to major status, given time.

Switzerland's only other "progressive" band, previous to Krokus, had been the jazz-rock ensemble Tea. And, to give some idea of the tight, near incestuous music scene there, Storace had been a member of that band too. Hair-splitters should note that Storace is from Malta — but he's spent the vast majority of his professional life in Switzerland or London.

The first murmurings of musical life from the Continent, other than pop or novelty records, was heard from the Netherlands and from Scandinavia.

Classical/jass/rock band Focus, featuring Jan Akkerman (guitar) and Thijs Van Leer (keyboards), were the heralds of the so-called Dutch invasion with single hits with "Sylvia" and "Hocus Pocus".

Fellow Dutch band Golden Earring represented the more metal orientated approach and made an immediate impact with the single "Radar Love". They were subsequently never to repeat that success, but remain an active unit to this day.

While Focus and Golden Earring were making their way at the beginning of the Seventies there were various Scandinavian outfits making noises. The more rock orientated bands were Denmark's Burning Red Ivanhoe, Finland's Tasvallan Presidentti and Norway's Jonas Fjeld Band. None of them have done anything of significance, from the international point of view.

It has been Germany which has offered up strong heavy metal bands from the European scene however, despite having a domestic rock market which dates back only about as far as 1968.

Through a mixture of indifference, lack of centralisation of the record industry and the curious effects of German anti-slavery laws (which happened to include band management as one of the prohibited practices) Germany was lucky to avoid having a still-born rock industry.

However, bands did emerge which began to garner international reputations. Most of them, though, were heavily influenced by experimentalism, jazz and avant-garde classicism — like Tangerine Dream, Can, Kraftwerk, Amon Düül II and Neu. Heavier orientated bands began to show through however, such as Birth Control and Frumpy (latterly known as Atlantis).

The biggest of the German bands to break were the Scorpions and by the beginning of this decade they were busily establishing themselves in the States, having already broken in Britain.

SCORPIONS

They have the benefit of a superb lead singer in Klaus Meine and an excellent guitarist in Rudolf Schenker — brother of the noted Michael Schenker who was instrumental in encouraging the band to try their hands in the big league of heavy metal.

Michael was originally a member of the Scorpions and joined UFO early in the Seventies. Having seen him do well in Britain the Scorps thought they had a chance too. And so they did, it subsequently proved. With albums like *Animal Magnetism* and *Love Drive* they've shown themselves as masterly exponents of mainstream metal.

The aforementioned Michael Schenker having left the Scorpions has formed his own band — called The Michael Schenker Band, with the first album produced by ex-Deep Purple ex-Rainbow member Roger Glover.

Other German bands beginning to make a noise are Lucifer's Friend (who include two Englishmen, singer Mike Starrs and keyboard player Adrian Askew) and Accept.

Having had a metal scene of no more than a handful of years' standing Germany looks poised to become a major force in the future.

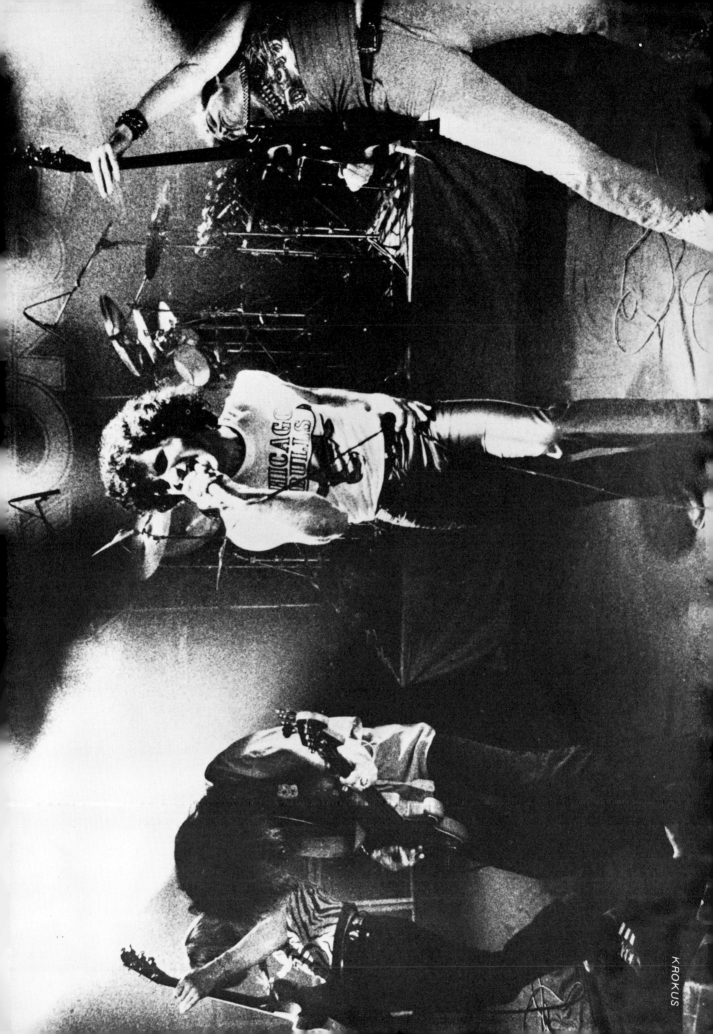

KROKUS

KLAUS MEINE

GETCHA ROCKS OFF. UK '76_'80

The rise of heavy metal during the final months of the Seventies in many surprising ways encapsulated the sad inevitability and inherent dangers that constantly lie dormant within the whole philosophy of rock 'n' roll fashion cycles. Why? Simply because when a musical force becomes merely translated into a trendy movement the whole process is destined to turn the wheel of change into a treadmill.

But to understand just why and how this took place in the case of the New Wave of British Heavy Metal (or NWOBHM for short), it really is necessary to look back at the rock scene some years previous. By 1975, mere fame and fortune had become insufficient elixirs to many performers; two decades of rock 'n' roll hedonism had begun to have a totally unexpected effect on the musicians within the menagerie. With the attraction of more and more articulate, intelligent artisans into the fray, the notion of 'respect' gradually started to erode that old show business catalyst of 'adulation', playing for the people took a poor second place to performing for the critics. Yet the only way to gain acceptance in higher circles was to take hold of the kicking, spitting brat that was rock 'n' roll and give it a thoroughbred art-form gloss. Words such as 'symphony', 'opera' and 'concerto' entered blithely into the text-book of contemporary jargon and musos became artists, LPs were converted into albums and the entire concept of 'hit singles' was at least temporarily discredited. Slowly thought-music was coming into vogue and length of works was regarded as more important than actual content. It was, of course, an isolationist principle that slowly but inexorably alienated the vast mass of the populus, particularly in the 16-18 year-old age bracket who had been attracted to rock 'n' roll in general and heavy metal in particular because it had a guttersnipe level of energy and intensity and because stars like Ozzy Osbourne were 'one of us'. By stripping the entire scene of such virtues, the *nouveau* academics were destroying the very essence of rock's appeal.

Punk (or new wave to give it a more generically correct term) arrived on the scene in late 1976 as the to-be-expected backlash against the gauche norm. When you have only one albeit limited weapon at your disposal (as so many perceived rock 'n' roll in the Fifties and Sixties) and this is suddenly neutralised by its protagonists (as had occurred by the mid-Seventies conversion of musicians into modern icons), then some form of radicalisation is inevitable. The emergence of a 'new order' dictated the need for a return to the grass-roots and the replacement of multi chord complexity with pure, unabashed NOISE. One-chord wonders sprung out of the woodwork everywhere repulsing the majority of 'punters' yet earning the unashamed adulation of the few to whom punk was a kick in the backside to the establishment that controlled the music business and all of its attendant outlets. Band names such as Strawberry Alarm Clock, Velvet Underground and Gryphon were superseded by the likes of the Clash, Damned and Slaughter & The Dogs as the greatest upheaval contemporary music had known since the days of Elvis gripped the nation. But with the increasing media coverage, punk soon became chic, losing its horrific overtones in the process and transmuting into a quaint anachronism, the midnight nightmare of spittin', revoltin' subversives being quietly converted into a mid-day merry fashion. Hit status for the Jam and Police soon had the entire genre on its last meaningful legs.

However, for all the eventual unfulfilled promise and hope of punk it did put spirit and energy back into rock and helped to initiate what was to follow it in the ears of the fashion-conscious, cycle-grasping rock 'n' roll business — HEAVY METAL. Oh, sure, HM never did really go away; like rockabilly and mod, even during the nadir of its so-called 'credibility', metallic mayhem still roamed the streets and record stores like an uncaged and unthethered stallion of the highway, refusing to lie down and take 'punishment' like a man. A hardcore, loyal following of some 50,000 fans ensured that even during the late Seventies gigs and record sales were favourable comparable to any other game. Is it really a coincidence that bands like Birmingham quintet Judas Priest, Aussie five-piece AC/DC and yet another UK five-man demolition unit in UFO all at last made significant breakthroughs over here? If you have any doubts about this, check out sales figures for *Stained Class*, *Let There Be Rock* and *Lights Out* respectively. By the summer of 1979, the collective atmosphere and mood within the musical sphere seemed right for a major rejunvenation of interest in the whole concept of HM; a catalyst, however, was badly needed, a young UK band to capture the imagination of the nation and turn the attentions of everyone into those emergent outfits slowly climbing out of the clubland pits. Certainly there were plenty of contenders. In London, Angel Witch (a five-piece at this particular

point in time, headed by guitarist Kevin Heybourne), Samson (in the stages of building a strong sense of image) and the embryonic Iron Maiden had been linked together in what was to become known as the travelling HM crusade, playing gigs throughout the country under the guidance of DJ Neal Kay; from Berkshire a trio by the appropriate name of Sledgehammer were beginning to receive ample press interest via their own self-financed Slammer Records single called "Sledgehammer" and in Birmingham, a quintet by the name of Jameson Raid were armed and ready to put in a bid with their own GBH Records EP, "Seven Days Of Splendour". But none of these quite fitted the bill and finally the hour brought forth the boys in the guise of Sheffield's five-piece foragers, Def Leppard who adapted the influences of Thin Lizzy, Rush and UFO to their own needs and happened to be the right outfit at the right time in the right place at the right age and, what's more they had product out in the form of a three-track self-financed Bludgeon Riffola EP featuring "Getcha Rocks Off" and "The Overture" as particular highlights, the former being a back-biting anthem and the latter a Rush-style epic. Not classical stuff by any means, yet this release did possess a naive charm and a quality that stood up and demanded to be noticed —

IRON MAIDEN

and was! Radio One DJs Andy Peebles and John Peel (the latter in many ways being the guru of the new wave) gave it plenty of valuable air-time and *Sounds*' heavy metal specialist Geoff Barton did a three-page interview on the band and suddenly the public bagan to take notice of the Yorkshire youngsters — the New Wave Of British Heavy Metal (a term devised and introduced by *Sounds*) had officially opened for trade.

Phonogram won a hard-fought battle for Def Leppard's highly-prized signature (a sum in the region of seven figures being rumoured as the final payment), EMI bagged the by-now fully-formed Iron Maidens and slowly many of the earlier exponents of the NWOBHM began to come under the lucrative spotlight shining out from the A&R departments of many major record companies.

Yet, strange things were most decidedly happening. For a start many newer outfits didn't immediately throw in their promising lot with the likes of CBS, Polygram or EMI as expected and the independent labels enjoyed a considerable upsurge. London-based melodic quartet Praying Mantis put out a three-track EP on Ripper Records entitled *Soundhouse Tapes, Vol Two*; the EF Band (a two-parts-Swedish-plus-one-part-English trio) and Pennines powerchord merchants Vardis (another trio) released singles on Shropshire label Redball, who had come to the fore during the punk era with efforts by such as the Not Sensibles and Vardis subsequently issued a second seven-incher on their own Castle Records; down in London town Samson put out their first album on   Lazer . A Brum quartet (who had actually been on the scene since the mid-Seventies and had an LP out on Jet in '77) re-jigged the old Mountain favourite ''Nantucket Sleighride'' for Reddington's Rare Records (based around a chain of four Midlands retail stores) and (by far the most productive label), in the North-east of England, Neat Records came into being originally via the debut single from the Tygers Of Pan Tang (a local outfit) and following this one's success (the title being ''Don't Touch Me There''), other bands in the area such as Fit, White Spirit and Raven also found the label of immense help in launching careers and now Neat claims with some justification to be the UK's leading independent HM label.

Sure, many of these outfits have since moved on to big name companies but the lesson of punk in the bold philosophy of small-time recordings done on the cheap being more than merely methods of attracting the unwilling attentions of the majors; they can be ways of making money in their own right. Equally as important, there seemed to be a strong bond linking together both the newer and older outfits. The likes of Leppard, Maiden and Samson toured with huge superbands of the calibre of AC/DC, Sammy Hagar, Judas Priest and Rainbow;

superficially, it seemed, things were progressing rather well.

However, no sooner had the media and the industry in general, realised that a veritable armada of new, fresh, young HM mavericks were on the loose than the whole 'experience' was translated into a bona fide 'movement' — and the seeds of doubt and destruction were sown. The problem quite simply was one of gross overgeneralisation. Of course, many bands did indeed fit snugly into the pigeon-hole characteristics of the much-publicised NWOBHM handle as seen by the press but equally a high number of others just didn't. The dilemma facing such protagonists as Praying Mantis (a high energy, melodically-based hard rock bunch), White Spirit (a keyboards-orientated quintet) and Money (a trio once dubbed by Neal Kay as more into hierarchy rock and NOT heavy metal) was: ''Do we accept being branded as metallic mayhem masters of reality because it's fashionable and therefore we stand a better chance of getting a deal plus work or alternatively, do we deny HM connections and risk being dumped?'' That so many worthy groups have

IRON MAIDEN

had their chances of 'making it' irrecovably decimated by the fundamentally limiting connotation of that term 'NWOBHM' is the first indictment against the entire concept of its perception as a movement. The second danger that quickly came to the fore within the NWOBHM ranks was that many of the young outfits were and still are unfit not to mention unprepared to face the sudden rush of acclaim that began to accompany their every move. Nowhere has this been better illustrated than in the case of Def Leppard. Their naivety in the shark-eat-dog world of rock very rapidly became obvious as they were reduced to the level of zombie pawns by those who surrounded and guided them. Nothing they've done since that near-legendary Bludgeon Riffola effort has even started to fulfill any inherent potential the band may possess. In short DL have advanced according to some master plan but certainly not grown up in any sense. They have allowed themselves to be strait-jacketed into a package aimed solely at the lucrative US market BEFORE gaining the lasting respect and adulation of home fans and their much-to-be-desired debut album *On Through The Night* needed the best producer money could buy in Judas Priest collaborator Tom 'Colonel' Allom to hide and smooth over the Leppard weaknesses and the entire sorry story reached a not-too-unexpected rock-bottom when, after months of US touring with the likes of Ted Nugent, Scorpions and Pat Travers, the young Sheffield outfit played at the 1980 Reading Festival and got an exceptionally hostile reception. There can surely be little doubt now that industrial requisites and the whole rock 'n' roll philosophy of, in the words of the New York Dolls, ''Too Much Too Soon''

ANGEL WITCH

has all but destroyed the very band who were hailed as messianic monarchs just 12 months previously.

Sadly, they aren't alone in HM circles and the survival rate is likely to prove very low indeed. But what of those who are capable of prospering and going on to achieve the greatness of a Led Zeppelin, Deep Purple, Black Sabbath, Cream or Hendrix? Clearly Saxon (who for years slogged away on the pub/club circuit as Son Of A Bitch) have now firmly established a sizeable niche for themselves and the enormous success of their second album for Carrere Records, *Wheels Of Steel* has set them up, one feels for a lifetime. Iron Maiden will also be around the top echelons for a long while yet and clearly look as if world-wide fame is theirs for the asking. But what of the rest? Vardis, now signed to Logo and with a successful tour as support to Hawkwind now behind them, will do very well as they've the sort of sound that will appeal to a wide cross-section of rock 'n' roll fans; White Spirit also have the makings of future heroes while Cheshire denizens Silverwing, with their penchant for brash US-style overkill on live shows have already made a good start in building up a strong national interest and any band who can come up with a single title like "Rock & Roll Are Four Letter Words" must be dead certs for the high life. But the three bands who should prove to be THE most significant to emerge from this whole escapade are Angel Witch, Girlschool and Diamond Head. The Witches now established as a hard-hitting trio have an almost unbelievable following of real fanatics and on the recording front have never failed to be less than 100 per cent compulsive.

Certainly it's to AW that those who go for a basically primitive yet highly proficient sound will turn in their thousands as the natural successors to Black Sabbath. Girlschool? This four-piece, no-nonsense all-female mob from South of the River Thames single - handedly changed the long-held view that girls can't really rock like pros and the enormous impact of their masterful first album for Bronze, *Demolition*, plus a stunning performance in July '80 at Motorhead's seven-band Bingley Hall extravaganza looks to have launched them into the megastar bracket. On the other hand, Stourbridge quartet Diamond Head have taken their time in thrusting into the limelight. First put together in 1977, the band steadily worked a passage across the UK, gaining fans everywhere on the strength of a sound that is a cross between Zeppelin and Sabbath and the release of two independent singles on Media Records in "Sweet & Innocent" plus its predecessor "Shoot Out The Lights" stirred up the scene in their favour. Now, they are slowly developing along highly individual and thoughtful lines moulding their approach into the sphere of sophisticated heavy rock and clearly they seem set to have a profound influence on future bands.

These eight aside, though, it does indeed look increasingly as if many bands will struggle to earn a crust and some might well succumb to the needs of the flesh and adapt their music to the prevailing winds of change.

Yet, if all of the preceding verbiage sounds just a mite on the bitter side then let it still be said that a number of lessons have been learnt from the trials and errors of the last couple of years. The enormous

DIAMONDHEAD

increase in bands prepared to commit themselves to vinyl at their own expense has meant that in a documentary sense at least they most certainly will not be lost to eternity and have secured at least in small measure a place in the rock 'n' roll hall of partial fame. Indeed, as an interesting sideline on the whole upsurge in cost-effective releases, two major companies went to the trouble of putting together compilation albums, containing demo tracks from a whole host of hopeful hammer-chordiacs. True, at the bottom of such behaviour was the urge to capture a slice of the action riding high on the crest of public interest at the start of 1980 in new, exciting HM heroes whilst at the same time not committing vast fortunes to any group before there had been business assessments made of potential future profits to be had from backing certain of them. Nevertheless, such LPs did also provide 'shop-windows' for unknowns who would otherwise have found it decidedly difficult to cut product and thence issue it to a mass market with the right sort of marketing approach.

Leading the way in this respect was, to many people's surprise, EMI via their *Metal For Muthas* series and indeed several of the bands show-cased on the two albums in this venture (each containing 10 numbers from nine bands) and a four-track EP have gone on to greater rewards as a result. From ''Vol One'', put into the racks in February of 1980, Iron Maiden are, as previously stated, now firmly ensconced in a stall at EMI's own stables (with top producer Martin Birch being lined up for their second album), Samson are signed up with Gem (who also have UK Subs and Canis Major, the latter being one of many bands attempting to fuse new wave and hard-rock dynamics), Angel Witch have linked up with Bronze (having followed up the appearance of ''Baphomet'' on the aforementioned LP by putting out a single in ''Sweet Danger'' on EMI which charted at number 75 in the BMRB singles run-down during June) and Praying Mantis, after releasing an abortive single on Gem in the eponymous ''Praying Mantis'' itself have an album

due out early in 1981 on Arista; oh yes and Nutz (one of many outfits whose embryonic battles for success were fought during the period when punk ruled the roost) have since changed their name to Rage, thrown in their lot with Carrere and subsequently released a seven-incher in ''Money'' and toured with Rory Gallagher. ''Vol Two'', put out in May, brought White Spirit and Dark Star (a five-piece from Birmingham, formerly known as Berlin) into the fray and the former are now with MCA whilst the latter are to be found on the roster of Alvin Lee's company Avatar, who also deal with Chevy (again first featured on ''Vol Two'').

Hot on the heels of EMI's example, MCA compiled a collection of 12 tracks in the same vein, featuring among others the myriad delights of Diamond Head, White Spirit and a duo of other North-eastern supremos in Fist (a quartet who initially came into favour via their debut single on

Neat Records ''Name, Rank & Serial Number'' and now themselves signed to MCA) and power-trio Raven plus Medway Towns four-piece May West and two bands also to be found contributing to the ''M For M'' series, London quartet Xero and that almost hardy perennial bunch from Berkshire, Sledgehammer. And as if these recordings weren't sufficient, Logo Records (who now boast Vardis and Germanic gargantuawatt gladiators Accept on the books) took up the rights to an album put together by Des Moines/Nigel Burnham (a *Sounds* writer) and featuring 16 bands nation-wide, including Vardis, Silverwing and an Essex quartet by the appropriately uncompromising name of Bastille; meantime the BBC raked up sessions first recorded for Tommy Vance's Friday Night Rock Programme and issued works from Samson, Praying Mantis, Angel Witch, Taurus (a five-piece straight-ahead in the boogie mould from Middlesborough), More (yet another quintet of straight-ahead motorised riff-mongers from London), Money and Trespass (a five-man crew of melodic heavy rockers from Suffolk also featured on *M For M, Vol Two*).

Yet, arguably, for all the importance of such LPs in bringing localised sounds out of geographical borders and spreading the word on a national scale, the most vital ramification to have shaken itself loose from the events of the past 24 months has been an increased acceptance of heavy rock at both club and pub level. Psychologically, many proprietors have now been 're-educated' into acknowledging that HM bands bring in considerable hard-core numbers, who don't create trouble

VARDIS

IRON MAIDEN

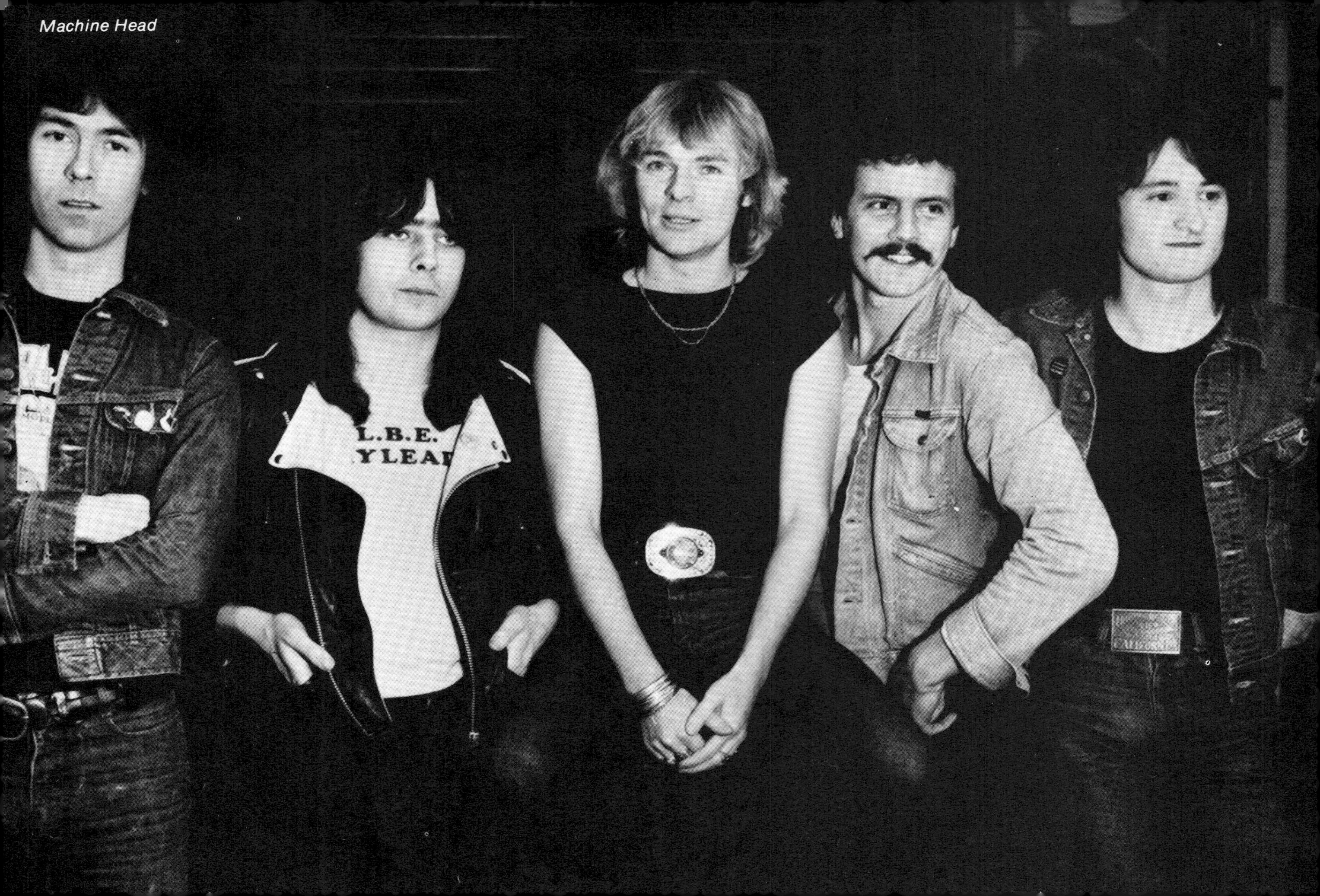

Machine Head

(despite the denim/leather uniform) of the inter-tribal kind so often associated with punk. Being able to put the music back on the streets, as it were, has certainly opened the previously locked gates to the countless numbers of young people with aspirations of mounting an axe attack in the true tradition of Jimmy Page or Angus Young or alternatively stretching the larynx à la David Coverdale or Klaus Meine; such a healthy situation must be good for the continual watering of the grass-roots in the right manner and thus ensure a constant stream of potential big-names through into the spotlight. Another firmly planted plank in the foundation comes courtesy of the HM discos up and down the country. It's a strange yet undeniable fact that national radio and television exposure has played virtually no part at all in the discovery of emergent talent (where is the HM answer to John Peel, for example?), rather directly on the scene in the clubs have taken up an altogether more central role. Places such as the Bandwagon in the heart of North-west suburban London, Crackers (situated not far from the capital's famous Marquee club) and Brolly's (right on the Thames in Richmond) have all made names for themselves providing live music from unknown bands plus airing new independant singles and demo tapes, thus giving the fans an immediate contact with what's actually happening, especially on a local level. Not only in London but all over the UK this has been going on with increasing regularity and the appearance of club-compiled HM charts in *Sounds* and *Record Mirror* has enabled these venues to gain in stature and no sign of a fall-off in interest is yet detectable.

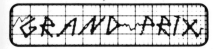

But what of the future? Can heavy metal truly ride out the backlash? Only time, of course, can really satisfactorily answer such a query but for all the cynicism and disappointments rife within the genre presently, there are encouraging pointers slowly creeping out of the swamps. In traditional British style, the scene is starting to diversify and expand its portfolio. The real heavy metal head-banging bands will always be with us (and long may that continue); Motorhead, More and another London 'shout it out LOUD' mob Weapon and their ilk will never lack for faithful followers. But elsewhere, keyboards-orientated-hard-rock as practised by the likes of White Spirit, Brummie sextet Cryer, Kentish three-piece Triarchy and RCA big hope Grand Prix is emergeing as a contender; heavy blues is back in vogue thanks to Diamond Head; metal/pop could soon be dominating the charts through the likes of Alien (a quintet from Leicester); the whole boogie area of rock, for so long solely the domain

of Status Quo, is far healthier at the moment as Taurus, Fist and Merseyside beasties Spider, begin to shape and mould their sound for the Eighties and hard-rock/new wave crossover appeal is working rather impressively in the capable hands of Scots high-flyers RAF, Midlands challengers Brooklyn and a couple of London-based outfits in Canis Major and Screen Idols.

But whatever the unpredictable future has planned for HM, nothing can take away from the sheer high-energetic, gut-bustin' rapid fire excitement that the NWOBHM gave to the UK at the close of one decade (the Seventies) and the opening of another (the Eighties). And if you disagree, why have you just spent valuable time reading a chapter specifically on the subject?

THE GREEDIES

JUDAS PRIEST

VARDIS